The Change⁹

Insights into Self-Empowerment

Jim Britt ~ Jim Lutes

With

Co-authors From Around the World

The Change⁹

Jim Britt ~ Jim Lutes

All Rights Reserved

Copyright 2015

The Change

10556 Combie Road, Suite 6205

Auburn, CA 95602

The use of any part of this publication, whether reproduced, stored in any retrieval system or transmitted in any forms or by any means, electronic or otherwise, without the prior written consent of the publisher, is an infringement of copyright law.

Jim Lutes ~ Jim Britt

The Change⁹

ISBN: 978-1-4951-8657-8

Co-authors

Richard Oden

Art Costello

Cheril Goodrich

Diana Scanlan

Diana Garber

Paul Lowe

Lyn Smith

Angie Taylor

Pennie Quaile-Pearce

Wendy Nagel

James King

Kathryn Wilking

Sherry Brantley

Sid Maestre

Patricia Rundblade

Kristin Marie Ecklund

Shelby Molchan

Peggy Sealfon

Frenee Dellosa

Mickell Rose

The Change is proud to support

Good Women International

Every five minutes, one American child (many as young as ten years old) will be abducted and trafficked into the sex trade. 274 children a day. 100,000 each year and that estimate could be low. The total current number of human trafficking victims in the U.S. alone reaches into the hundreds of thousands and worldwide into the millions.

All profits from the sale of Amazon Kindle electronic books are being donated to Good Women International, whose focus is on the prevention of sexual exploitation of young women and children. They support self-empowerment and educational programs worldwide designed to educate our youth to avoid becoming a victim. A recent successful project was an anti-trafficking curricula for our high schools which is now complete.

Enslavement is a reality. It is documented and it is real. The question is: What are we going to do about it?

To make a donation to Good Women International, a non-profit subsidiary of Village Care International, go to: www.SupportGoodWomen.com. All donations are tax deductible under Tax ID #: 88-0471768. We welcome and appreciate your donations no matter how small.

http://GoodWomenInternational.org

Note: *Donations are never for salaries, as Good Women is a volunteer organization*

DEDICATION

This book is dedicated to all those seeking change

Foreword

Berny Dohrmann, Chairman of CEO Space International

To The Readers of *The Change* Series:

Jim Britt has been a mentor to *Chicken Soup* authors, and to some of the foremost thought leaders on earth. Jim Britt's groundbreaking work in *Letting Go*, releasing past traumas and betrayals in life to return once again to forward-looking manifestation within your full powers, has been instructing at leading *Fortune* companies and to standing-room-only seminars all over the world. For three decades, Jim Britt has been the "trainer of the trainers," of which I am only one. Jim has been an instructor at CEO Space, the most prestigious, hard to get into faculty on the planet, where he developed millions of dollars of resources as he assisted others to develop tens of millions of dollars for their own dream making. Jim is the most "unchanged by success and wealth" man I have ever known. He is an unselfish archangel, like in his book *Rings of Truth*.

Today, Jim Britt and Jim Lutes, along with many inspiring co-authors from around the world, bring a pioneering work to the market to transform your own journey into master manifestation. Their principles are forged on coaching millions on every continent. As you read, you are exploring self-development as the world has yet to practice. In fact, Jim and Jim's publications lead to this one APEX MOMENT. Everything you have done to date in your own life, everyone you have met, every lesson you have learned, has led you to this one GREAT life opportunity… the moment of your own transformation into ever-rising full potentials.

As a five-time best-selling author myself, as a filmmaker, and with CEO Space, you can imagine how fussy I am to write a foreword to publications in the self-development space. CEO Space was just ranked by *Forbes Magazine* as the leading entrepreneur firm, which hosts five annual business growth conferences serving over 140 countries. It was also named by *Forbes* as THE MEETING in the world that YOU CANNOT AFFORD TO MISS. The world today demands more than a reputation defender to secure your forward brand; it requires that you take responsibility for your own brand and reputation in life. This book will inspire you to do just that.

CEO Space International has supported launches for many amazing works, including *Chicken Soup for the Soul; Men Are From Mars, Women Are From Venus; Rich Dad, Poor Dad; The Secret; No Matter What; Three Feet From Gold; Conversations With The King;* and now the movies *Growing Up Graceland* and *Wish Man* (for Make a Wish Foundation); *Outwitting the Devil* by Napoleon Hill and Sharon Lechter; Tony Robbins' great publications; of course Jim Britt's best-selling book *Rings of Truth;* and so many more. The totals have reached more than 2 billion eyeballs! You can't play around with that Mount Everest of credibility that I guard like a bank vault!

You can therefore appreciate why I encourage 100% of our followers of all the publications named to BUY JIM BRITT and JIM LUTES' book series *The Change* as a customer recognition for your own ten-best close relationships or clients. But don't just buy this book; rather, I endorse that you buy 10, and you giftwrap them to acknowledge your most important top ten relationships in life or clients in business. By doing so, you will retain more clients and encourage repeat buying. You may also receive more referrals and strengthen each relationship. The laws of giving will come back to you 10 to 1. When you give freely, you will always receive a rain into your life just as you rain into the lives of those you treasure. Jim Britt, Jim Lutes, and the insightful and inspiring co-authors have given you in *The Change* series a great opportunity… more important than pouring ice water over someone's head on YouTube as a challenge for charity! The gift that keeps on giving begins when you step up and BUY 10, knowing you have been instrumental in inspiring 10 friends to live a better life. Together, we are going to reach 1 BILLION SOULS as we help Jim Britt, Jim Lutes, and their co-authors to achieve their goal to transform human consciousness in our lifetime. Like Zig Ziglar, Jim Rohn, the great Roger Anthony, and so many friends who have passed, my friend Jim Britt is now a historical event in every training, every publication, and every online work at CEO Space. If you ever have the opportunity, STOP YOUR LIFE and see JIM BRITT & JIM LUTES LIVE and you will thank me personally, I know.

Their work is powerful. You'll let go of the baggage you've been carrying around for years and learn to embrace everything that creates the future you want and deserve. As you close the pages of any of *The Change* books, you will say over and over again "THANK YOU Jim Britt and Jim Lutes for creating this work." You will gain a new life of super focus as never before and you will commence to master manifest in your own individual life as never before. *The Change* books provide tools to transform results for corporations, institutions, and individuals, and once applied it will be impossible to miss your future success in life.

In my opinion, there are only the following areas to embrace for each of us:

Spiritual oneness and balance

Recreational balance and nature

Relationship where *Perfection Can Be Had!* (my book)

Career attainment of goals that you, yourself, reset along the way

Parenting either directly or by embracing a child you adopt to mentor at any and every age in life

These perspectives come into alignment within a framework of Jim Britt and Jim Lutes' imagination, along with decades of human-potential work. My advice is this work is a "BUY 10 TO SHARE WITH FRIENDS" pledge. In fact, a billion readers is a global path that Jim Britt and Jim Lutes are going to achieve NEXT for the world common good.

Let's help in this quest, as both men unselfishly donate their only asset, their precious LIFE TIME, to elevate one life at a time to their full potential and greatness.

My final request to all those who are reading my foreword is that you DO IT NOW. When you think of the good you will be doing, just ask yourself, "How long will I make them WAIT?"

I'm buying my 10 today!

Berny Dohrmann

Chairman, CEO Space International

P.S. I so approve this message for all my readers and followers worldwide. CEO Space has helped authors break the book of all records a half a dozen times, which means the only record to beat can be done with the publication you are buying 10 of now. Together, we are going to set a global record with one publication. Make the PLEDGE and give the gift of personal development. DO IT TODAY!

Table of Contents

Foreword vii

Jim Britt 1
    The Truth about Success

Jim Lutes 13
    Inside the Vault

Angie Taylor 23
    Make it Simple - Live in Wellness Daily

Art Costello 33
    What's Possible

Cheril Goodrich 45
    On the 8th Day

Diana Garber 57
    Three Powerful Words

Diana Scanlan 65
    Heal Yourself, Heal the Planet: How personal change will increase planetary harmony

Frenee Dellosa 77
    Free your mind right now!

Dr. James R. King 89
    In Search of Humanity's Vision: Where Do We Go From Here?

Kathryn Wilking 103
    The Fantastic Five: Find the Answers, Get the Advantage

Kristin Marie Ecklund 115
    Three Keys to Unlock Your Inner Genius

Lyn Smith 127
   Survive, Heal, & Thrive 'Rape & Sexual Abuse'

Patricia A. Rundblade 139
   Journey of a Hero: Revealing the Hero Within

Peggy Sealfon 149
   An Integrated Life Is the Way to Authentic Success

Paul Lowe 161
   From Forest Wilderness to Global Contribution

Pennie Quaile-Pearce 175
   Breathe The Change

Richard A. Oden 187
   Uncovering Your Greatness

Shelby Molchan 201
   Would You Change To Save Your Life?

Sherry Brantley 211
   Change The Beliefs That Keep You In Grief

Wendy Nagel 221
   The World needs a Potential Revolution

Sidney Maestre 235
   I AM THAT I AM

Mickell Rose 247
   Take Care of Your Body So That Your Mind Will Awaken Your Soul

Afterword 257

Jim Britt

Jim Britt is an internationally recognized leader in the field of peak performance and personal empowerment training. He is author of 13 best-selling books, including *Cracking the Rich Code; Cracking the Life Code; Rings of Truth; The Power of Letting Go; Freedom; Unleashing Your Authentic Power; Do This. Get Rich-For Entrepreneurs; The Flaw in The Law of Attraction;* and *The Law of Realization,* to name a few.

Jim has presented seminars throughout the world sharing his success principles and life-enhancing realizations with thousands of audiences, totaling over 1,000,000 people from all walks of life.

Jim has served as a success counselor to over 300 corporations worldwide. He was recently named as one of the world's top 20 success coaches and presented with the best of the best award out of the top 100 contributors of all time to the direct selling industry. He also mentored/coached Anthony Robbins for his first five years in business.

Jim is more than aware of the challenges we all face in making adaptive changes for a sustainable future

The Truth about Success

By Jim Britt

In order to attain a different result, you have to do something differently, wouldn't you agree? And, in order to do something different, you must first know something different to do. Is that not true?

It's impossible to know what you don't know, or to change if you don't know how to change. Which brings up my next point. In order to know something different to do, you must first suspect that your present method needs improving. That's called awareness. If you want to change, you must first become aware that you may need to do something in a different way.

Years ago, I was interviewing a young man for a commission sales job. I asked him what income he was looking to earn his first year or two. He said that he wanted to earn $100,000 his first year and at least a 50% increase his second year. Then I asked him what was the highest income that he had ever earned in a single year. He answered, *"$20,000."* Next, I asked him if he thought he was worth $100,000 a year. He answered hesitantly, "I don't know. I think so." My last and most important question was, "What do you plan to change about yourself to go from a $20,000 a year earner to a $100,000 a year earner, and then to a $150,000 a year earner?" His answer was, "I don't know."

My point is this: as long as he considers himself to be a $20,000 a year income earner, he will never become a $100,000 a year income earner. There is always something that needs changing in order to make advancements. Maybe it's simply having a new opportunity available and getting inspired by that opportunity. Maybe it's a matter of focus and being fully committed to something. Maybe it's learning and applying some new concepts or ideas. Maybe it's improving your personality or people skills. Maybe there is a need to be more self-confident or to simply have the courage to take a risk. Maybe there is a need to hire a mentor or coach. Or maybe there is a need to change one or more self-limiting beliefs, or to let go of some fear.

Your income or your personal development will rarely exceed your beliefs. Your income will rarely exceed your personal growth. Your income will rarely exceed your ability to see a need for improvement. And if it does on some rare occasion, it will quickly come back to where it was in a short period of time if you don't make a change along with it.

It is impossible to achieve the next level of success with the same thinking, beliefs, and behaviors that brought you where you are today. This is why it is critical to have a plan for your own growth. Otherwise, you'll continue to produce the same results you've always produced.

There is no system that I, or anyone else, could offer to change anyone's perceptions unless they thought it needed improving and were open to a better way. As an example, if I believe a certain thing to be true or if I believe that my way is the only way, then I will be heavily invested in protecting my belief.

But on the other hand, if I remain *open* to learning better, more efficient methods, if something or someone wakes me up to the truth or to a better way and I discover that I do in fact have a choice, I then free myself to look with a new perspective and to make changes.

Your beliefs are always what holds you back. For example, you may be experiencing being broke, therefore you say, *"I am broke!"*

Or you may possess a certain degree from college, let's say in psychology; therefore, you say, *"I am a psychologist."*

Or you may say, *"I resent successful people."* Therefore, *"I am resentful."*

Or you may say, *"Earning money is difficult."* Therefore, it will be difficult for you

These are all beliefs. And a belief is not the same for any two people. A belief is something that *you* decide is true. The reality is that it may not be true at all. It's simply your opinion. In fact, when you really look at it, all beliefs are false. A belief you hold is only something that you have decided is true…it is simply your perception or truth.

Our beliefs have become so imprinted on our self-identity that we have built powerful support systems to reassure one another that what we do and what we have is who we are. We seem to always want to change outside circumstances, change other people, change the government, change our relationship, change our job, and so on, in an attempt to change our lives.

Some think that if they have a good enough reason for *not* succeeding, they can avoid taking a risk or stepping out of their comfort zone. So they use a smokescreen of excuses designed to distract themselves and others from the real truth…which is that they haven't taken enough action to even get started.

Some use being in a state of emotional upheaval as an excuse. "If I'm upset, you can't expect me to be responsible for my results." Being the victim is often a common reason used for explaining away lack of results. Being a victim is simply a belief. And it's a belief that can be changed.

You can take this to the bank. Your beliefs have total control over your life.

You can also take this to the bank. You have total control over what you believe.

You've no doubt heard the saying, *"seeing is believing."* But the reality is that believing is not true seeing. Believing may not be seeing the truth at all. In fact, it could be the opposite. Direct experience is the only way to know the truth.

Let's say you are in sales. What sort of results would you produce if you talked to 100 new prospects this month about your business or product? You might believe, *"Well I might close 10% or 20%."* Or you might be thinking, *"A hundred people? I could never talk to a hundred people in a month. I don't even know a hundred people."* But the real *truth* is that you won't know for sure until you do it, will you?

People fail because they buy into the wrong story, the wrong belief. They buy into their own story, their false beliefs! That's the real truth that everyone deals with. Failure is self-imposed by how you *believe* and so is success. Going beyond belief and seeing the truth behind your beliefs is where success at anything starts. Knowing the real reasons for not achieving the level of success that you want up to this point, should that be the case, will help you to adjust the actions you take to produce the results you want.

Those who learn to see the truth behind their actions, to know reality…those who are willing to let go of old habits, to let go of the past, are in the best position to experience success. The past is what holds you back in the present. I'm not saying to forget the past, but simply remembering that the past is over is a good place to start.

The past is not the present and the past has no basis for reality in the present. What I'm saying is that the results you did or didn't produce yesterday do not count today. Whether your past was filled with success and victory or failure and loss, the past is not the present. And the present is not the past. Today is today. Only today will you achieve success today. If something negative happened to you in the past, get over it! Move on! Don't let it hold you back! It's not happening to you now unless you let it.

The Change[9]

To change your feeling or belief about a current condition, you don't need to analyze it to death any more than to deflect an avalanche do you need to know which snowflake was the first to start tumbling down the mountainside. In an avalanche, it's what's happening here and now that counts, isn't it? The only thing you need to know is *get out from under it!* It's what you're doing here and now that counts, not what happened in the past.

The only roadblock to success at anything is your old habits, especially if you don't realize that they're there. That's why it's so important to see the truth behind your circumstances instead of using them as an excuse for not living up to your full potential.

Ask yourself, "What am I hanging on to from the past that's keeping me from being all I can be now?"

I'm not talking about using *self-improvement, positive thinking, motivation, or some Law of Attraction method.* What I'm talking about is *self-observation, self-correction, correct thinking* and *correct action based on what's really happening.* Self-improvement is self-addition. Positive thinking is covering up the truth with *frills* and *glitter*. Motivation is called suppressing reality. Law of Attraction without correct action is just an exercise in mental gymnastics. They all give us a false sense of self by replacing reality with where we *wish* we were. If those things could have worked to produce success, everyone would be living the life of their dreams by now, don't you think? We've all had enough positive thinking and motivation to last a lifetime! What we need is *waking up, correct thinking* backed up by *correct action based on truth.*

This method of self-change can be carried out by you alone. It does not require a therapist. You don't need one at all. No one can do it for you. An analyst won't find anything that you can't find. In the end, it's just like this book. Each co-author can offer ideas for change, but they can't change you. Only you can change you.

Success at anything is about re-creating or re-inventing yourself moment to moment. Self-creation is a basic principle at work at every moment of your life. It's behind the creation of your personality, behind the creation of your mindset, your business, your success, your health, your relationships, and everything else in your life.

Every time you act, you add strength to the motive that's behind what you've done. For example, if the salesperson makes a presentation just for the sake of making a presentation and they are expecting to get a *no* because they've been getting *no's* all day, they actually reinforce the idea that they're going to receive another *no*. That's reality.

Inside your brain, you have little memory channels called dendrites. They look like the roots of a tree. Every time you think a new thought, you create a new root on the tree. And every time you rethink a thought, you strengthen the root that is already in place. It's called subconscious programming.

Let's say for instance that you are in a financial slump. If you continue to think you are in a slump and remain there long enough, you could develop and strengthen a program that you are not worthy of making money in the first place. Every time you act upon that belief or program, the underlying motive behind it is intensified. It can be an idea about money, about yourself, about others, about success, your abilities, or about the world. Whatever it is, it is intensified when you act upon it. The act retypes the message in your mind. It strengthens your dendrites. I guess you could call success and failure a *battle of the dendrites.*

You have to win the war against old habits in order to experience something new.

There's no room for both on the playing field. You *decide* to have one or the other. Which one have you *decided* to have?

Now, I don't want you to think that this is going to be complicated, even though it may sound so. Hey, I'm a high school dropout, so I'll keep it simple. Here's the key to winning the battle. When the message you receive is *"I don't deserve success,"* or whatever, and it isn't acted upon, it becomes weaker, as if fading from a movie screen. When it is acted upon, it becomes clearer and brighter, which will prompt more of the same. And if you've made a firm decision that doesn't allow for retreat, you will know which direction to take at every moment.

The most important factor here is to begin to recognize the truth behind your actions so that you know what the connection is between the decision, the act, and the result. You are in complete control here. You get to decide to let go of an old belief and let it wither away from lack of attention.

It's much like having a disease and you don't know the cure. I guess you could call the disease *paranoia*. The person with the disease is always worried. He thinks there's a conspiracy against him. He senses certain weaknesses in himself and he thinks everyone knows it. He thinks that everyone is out to see him fail. But don't worry. Everyone is too concerned about their own perceived weakness to notice yours anyway!

So where does this *paranoia* come from? Well if you have it, it came from you! That's called reality. That's called seeing the truth. You may not like the truth or even believe it to be the truth. But the truth is if you have the disease, you gave it to yourself. And only you can take it away. Paranoia is the self-creation principle at work in a very observable form. We all know about destructive habits because we all have them. And every time you indulge a destructive habit, you strengthen a dendrite, and with that comes its eventual greater grip creating more and more paranoia.

How do you stop this paranoia? By finding the action or habit that reinforces your fear and refraining from it. You must challenge the belief that is underlying "What do I believe about success, money, or whatever?"

"How did I come to believe this?"

"What if it's not true?"

"Who taught me to believe this way?"

"What if they didn't know the truth?"

"Is it reality?" And more importantly…"Who would I be without this belief?"

Ask yourself. *"Is there any reason that isn't painful or stressful to hang on to this belief?"* If not, let it go and move on.

Most important is that you must be willing to *observe* yourself and look for the truth. You have to be willing to look for the truth behind your actions and circumstances and take full responsibility for changing them. Once you see the truth, you now have to make the choice to cease to act in ways that reinforce the unwanted habit or belief…and to act in ways that will move you toward your desired outcome.

Let's say for example that you worry all the time about what people might think of you. What could you do instead of worry? How about nothing! And will doing nothing help ease the worry? Of course it will! On the other hand, if there is an action you could take, let go of your fear and take action. If there is no action you could take to resolve a problem, then simply let go and do nothing. When you let go, you weaken the habit.

Defending or justifying your belief will only increase your belief and strengthen the habit. When you take a chance and let go, it's true that you might have to face an emotional challenge. But you'll find that it's much better than spending your whole life on guard worrying about getting hurt. That's even worse, in my opinion, than actually getting hurt. But when you act with strength and courage, you will reinforce that premise.

Self-knowledge is the beginning of wisdom and transformation. Self-knowledge cannot be given to you by learning a system or from someone else. You must discover it for yourself. If your intention to know yourself is weak, then just a casual wish or hope to change is of very little significance. All transformation begins with self-knowledge and truth. Without knowing who you are and the truth behind your actions, there is no foundation for correct thinking. There is no reality. Without a foundation for correct thinking based upon self-knowledge and truth, there can be no correct action. Without correct action, there can be no change.

Truth is the starting point. Have you ever heard the statement *"The truth will set you free?"* The truth begins with the understanding of that which you are without distortion. That's what the statement means. It is not referring to merely telling the truth, although that's a good place to start, but rather understanding or seeing the truth.

Seeing the truth is where transformation begins. In fact, that's the only place it can begin. Truth gives you true freedom. Truth comes from the understanding of *what is* without distortion. Whereas when you're working toward change using some system that someone else has created for you to follow, or through *"motivation"* or *"positive thinking,"* that's called *postponement*. That's called the cover-up of *what is* with what you would like it to be.

Remember, the truth is that a belief is something that you have decided is true. It's a made-up story. It's a decision to think and act in certain ways. So how do you change a belief? You simply make up a different story.

***

To Contact Jim:

www.JimBritt.com

www.PowerOfLettingGo.com

www.CrackingTheRichCode.com

www.FaceBook.com/JimBrittOnline

www.JourneyBeginsNow.com

Jim Lutes

Having taught his branded form of human performance since the early 1990s, Mr. Lutes has accelerated top-level entrepreneurs throughout his career by conducting trainings on personal growth and subconscious programming into worldwide markets.

During this time, Jim took his skills regarding the human mind, and combining it with trainings on influence, persuasion, and communication strategies, he launched Lutes International in the early 1990s. Based in San Diego, California, Jim has taught seminars for corporations, sales forces, individuals, and athletes. Having appeared on television, radio, and worldwide stages, Jim's style, knowledge, and effectiveness provide profound results.

"Jim Lutes possesses a unique ability to create performance change in an individual in a fraction of the time it takes his competitors." The core of humans decisions are based on the programs we acquire, reinforce, and grow. Combining Jim's various trainings, individuals can reach new levels of achievement and fulfillment in all areas of life. The results are at times nothing short of astonishing.

Inside the Vault

By Jim Lutes

Every day, in virtually everything we do, there exists the internal/external dichotomy. Things truly are never what they seem. Rarely do we get access to the deeper workings of the person, event, place, or activity we are with, engaging in, taking part in. We tend to hang out on a very superficial plane of existence the majority of the time, focusing on how we look, judging others by how they look, and focusing on our physical bodies, but not our true selves—the parts on the inside that feel and think. For some people, they may not even know that they are in possession of all of the innate wisdom of the universe in their minds. So many people barely use a fraction of their brain power, and still others will live their whole lives unaware completely of the power they have had all along; power that is inherent within the subconscious mind. Remember, the subconscious mind connects to the expression of Universal Power.

Just like when you go into a bank and see the desks, chairs, and bank tellers when you enter, but you do not see the vault where the money is hidden, so it is with our own vault. People see each other on a physical level, and see themselves on a physical level, and don't look deeper into the vault of others, or their own vault—in this case, the subconscious mind. What's worse is that so many people don't even know this vault exists! When you go to a bank, you are aware that what you are seeing is not the money or the gold; you know that the money and the gold exist in a special vault that is accessed in a specific way by specific people. It's time to think of your subconscious mind as that same kind of special vault, and only you can access it. In that vault is stored a treasure trove of freedom, wealth, good health, great relationships—you name it, you can access it in your vault. The subconscious mind contains access to everything you need—everything you need to be healthy, to be happy, to be wealthy, to have the things you want in life. Most people don't even know about the existence of the subconscious mind, not to mention the power it contains.

Your vault is your subconscious mind, and it is where you are connected to Universal Power. Your subconscious mind is full of more wisdom, connection and knowledge than you can even begin to fathom. While everyone sees the external you, your version of the nice chairs and desks and bank tellers, the power that is inside your vault is what is driving this external you. It is vital to first of all understand that you have unlimited power within you to create the life of your dreams, and second of all to understand that regardless of whether or not you know this, whatever is inside your vault has already been driving the external you. Wouldn't you like to switch places and get behind the steering wheel for a change?

The vault of your subconscious mind is full of potential. The subconscious mind is the seat of Universal Power. We are connected to all the knowledge in the universe through our subconscious mind. We are beings of creation and all we really want to do is create and expand, much like the universe that we are a part of does inherently. We cannot do this if we are constantly disregarding our dreams, intuitions, gut feelings, or callings and instead spending all our days wrapped up in intellectualizing everything we do. I am not saying you must get spiritual and activate your pineal gland or even meditate daily. You don't need to believe in God, even. But believing that there is a higher power in the universe and that you are one with that higher power through your subconscious mind can be helpful when you start getting serious about getting rid of fears, doubts, limiting thoughts, and long-running programs. It is this sense of connection to a larger existence that can remind us of our healthy place in the rich context of all things. We are all connected to that Ocean of Universal Power!

Further to what we agreed the subconscious mind to be earlier, another analogy I like to use when talking about the subconscious mind is to liken the subconscious as the hard drive to the computer that is your conscious mind. The subconscious stores all kinds of information that otherwise clutters up the conscious mind. The conscious mind is the source of logic, reason, and rational thought. Anything that you take in that cannot be processed by the conscious mind is integrated in the subconscious mind. This includes traumatic experiences, visual images, and virtually all information taken in through the senses. The subconscious mind stores this information, to be used in your life at any time, or to present itself to you when the need arises. Often, the subconscious mind will use the information it has stored to warn you, or trigger you, or sometimes it will bring this information to your attention even when you have no idea what the connection or need might be behind it. Remember, the subconscious mind wants to protect you; it wants you to survive your life experiences.

The subconscious mind also controls all the functions of the body. Take a deep breath right now. How you take this breath when you are using your conscious mind is very different from just breathing. Your subconscious mind plays a part in keeping you breathing without thinking about it, all day long. When you are sleeping, the subconscious keeps you breathing. Now, sitting still, accelerate your heart rate. Go ahead—accelerate your heart rate. Were you able to do it? Chances are you weren't. This is because you are hearing the request and responding to it on a conscious level. You cannot consciously direct your subconscious to alter the way your body is functioning. However, if you dream you are being chased by a tiger, your heart rate will go up, you'll start to sweat, perhaps even awaken in the middle of the night. These bodily functions were activated by the subconscious in response to the images your dreaming mind presented to it. The subconscious keeps you functioning and safe on the physical level.

Another example: If you eat a poisonous food, your subconscious mind is what leads the physical response to throw the poisonous food up so it doesn't stay in your body. There are all kinds of examples of the subconscious mind taking information and letting us perform activities without having to think about them. Driving a car is a great one—when you first learned to drive a car, you were likely very conscious of how to put your foot on the brake or the clutch, how to hold the steering wheel, how to shift gears. Think about how you drive your car now, however. Sometimes I will be halfway out of the driveway before I even need to bring my conscious attention to what I am doing! After so many years of driving, my subconscious mind has learned all of the moves and actions so that I can get into my car, put the key in the ignition, and get driving without consciously having to think about any of the actions involved. This is like those habit patterns formed from early conditioning I mentioned earlier. Think about it—we drive and talk to people, we drive and fiddle with the stereo, we drive and eat! All that time, we are consciously talking to people, changing the music or eating—which means that the information about driving stored in our subconscious mind is what is actually letting the driving happen.

The subconscious mind is the conduit to Universal Power, and is a reminder that you are made up of this Universal Power. The subconscious mind wants to manifest outwardly everything that it receives from you inwardly. That is to say, what you think will be expressed; this is part of the mandate of the subconscious. The subconscious mind, backed by Universal Power, and the nature of the universe as creation, just wants to create for you that which you desire. Which is why it is essential to be aware of your thoughts and choose to think in ways that attract to you what it is you want. Imagine knowing you have access to Universal Power (and Universal Power is really what drives the universe as the ultimate creator), backing you up as you strive to achieve your goals in life! My world-class subconscious mind programming techniques can help you get to this knowing—and get to a place where you make an ally of your subconscious mind.

We are born with a blank canvas that is quickly imprinted with all the thoughts, fears, and beliefs of the influential figures around us as we grew up. Using subconscious mind programming techniques allows you to step out of the imprint on an emotional level so that you can no longer be held back by all of the clutter that has built up throughout your life in your subconscious mind. While you may never really empty the hard drive that is the subconscious mind, you can disable the power of the emotion connected to all that is stored within it. What I am saying is that you can't change your earlier experiences, but you can alter the way you relate to them. A strong emotion is what you are responding to when you are self-sabotaging, or old patterns resurface, or even unexplained fears or reactions to things take hold. If you have found yourself feeling anxious without really knowing why, or have fears that you can't understand why you have them, this is because the subconscious has a memory of an event and it is hanging on to this memory, and the original emotion that developed with it. The subconscious mind may be triggered by something in your conscious present that invokes the emotion of the event; even if you never knew or don't remember what that event is, you will feel this feeling and it could seriously hinder your life if it comes at the wrong time.

This part of the mind is truly locked away and very few people even know to access it in their lives, much less *how* to access it. Accessing your vault allows you to see what is stored there, and then clear the aspects that are no longer serving you. With this clearing, the vault can be unlocked, allowing you to access Universal Power and your own limitless potential. The subconscious mind is available to help maintain your body in good health. The subconscious mind is ready to help you become a millionaire by drawing money to you. The subconscious mind is ready to help you navigate your relationships so they become excellent relationships. The subconscious mind wants you to be an aligned human being so you can best serve the people around you and fulfill your mission as a part of creation in the universe. The subconscious mind is the universe working through you as a human. Are you starting to feel just how important the subconscious is—and how essential it is to have as an ally?

All you need to do is to unlock the subconscious mind—unlock your vault, as it were. The subconscious mind programming techniques were designed through my years of working in personal development as ways to help you unlock the vault so you can really get into the riches that are stored in it. These techniques are designed to take a look at what is in there, and then get to work on eradicating the emotion that limits you.

The subconscious mind is the most powerful part of our existence as humans. It really is our own vault where the real gold and riches are stored. Grasping the depth of potential that every human has inside of them is essential for moving forward into your life masterpiece. There is no need to fix anything, there is no need to add anything, you have all the answers that you seek. You just need a push in the right direction. That direction is reprogramming the subconscious, and I can show you how. If you knew that you had the power all along within you, would you not want to know how to access it to make your life better in every way imaginable? To align your life so that everything runs smoothly, from good health and financial success to great relationships and a sense of peace and well-being? This is what reprogramming your subconscious mind can do for you. We are the creators of our lives, for better and for worse, and the more you are able to recognize this, the more you can create the life of your dreams. The more you understand that life happens right now, not tomorrow, not some day, but right now, the more you will be inspired to take action. Taking action is integral in achieving results. If you are always procrastinating and postponing things, even if you feel motivated and are applying all the techniques discussed in this book, you are not actually taking action. Action is the essential piece in the puzzle of creating your life, manifesting your desires, and accomplishing great feats. By action, I mean implementing change in your daily life habits. You can change your subconscious programming all you want, but without also taking action and stepping fully into your life, you simply will not see results. It is pivotal that you apply the results of your 'changed' subconscious in your everyday lived experiences.

Procrastination only serves fear, and keeps you stuck in the life you are outgrowing as you become more aware. Imagine if Henry Ford had procrastinated or postponed his idea for making an automobile—cars nowadays might only look like they did in the sixties. We certainly would not have the electric car, and we may not have cars at all! Imagine if Bill Gates had procrastinated on creating Microsoft, or Steve Jobs postponed creating Apple, computer technology would be nowhere near what it is today. Each one of us is a unique and gifted soul with treasures to share with our families, our friends, our colleagues, indeed, with the world. When you procrastinate, you prevent yourself from sharing with anyone. How can you expect the accolades to come tumbling in when you postpone sharing what you are with the world?

Developing awareness about how you live each day is the best way to overcome these tendencies to procrastinate and postpone. We need to be constantly in a state of awareness, always on the lookout for what impedes progress in our lives. Is your life in perfect alignment? If any aspect of your life is out of kilter, be it your relationships, health, or financial well-being, then every aspect is affected, whether you are aware of this or not. If you are not aware of what is out of kilter, then you cannot bring everything back into alignment. However, if you know right away that your health is off and that this is affecting your relationships and financial situation, then you can take the necessary steps to bring everything back into order.

Consider the entrepreneur—entrepreneurs are another good example of people living in a state of awareness daily. Every entrepreneur knows that it is in their best interest to stay aware, so that if opportunities present themselves they can then adjust their lives to take advantage of these opportunities. In the event they may need to make quick decisions, by remaining aware an entrepreneur can seize any opportunity at a moment's notice. We can learn a lot from this type of approach to life. There is a necessary sense of urgency that we would do well to apply to life that helps us realize the value inherent in each day, hour, and minute.

We are all dying, from the moment we are born. There will never be a perfect time for anything. Life is full of broken fingers, broken hearts, broken cars, and some of the biggest regrets people have faced throughout the century have been around not doing something while they still had the chance. It is all too easy, especially in our culture of "work until you're 65, then retire and see the world" to remain rooted in procrastination and postponement, waiting for that magic "someday" to appear. This will only serve to limit you from experiencing life in a deep and rich way. Why wait until you're 65 to start living? Why wait until tomorrow, for that matter? Life is here right now, in this moment, as you read this book. What is it you most want to do? Ask yourself honestly, what are your deepest desires? You may feel limited by money, sure, this is common, and it might be your reality at the moment. But you are truly not limited by time, regardless of the story you tell yourself around time and what time is available to you.

***

To contact Jim:

Email: info@lutesinternational.com

Websites: www.lutesinternational.com

www.jimluteslive.com

Angie Taylor

Angie Taylor is a Doctor of Natural Health, Life Coach, Intuitive Eating Counselor, Speaker, and Author. She is considered by many to be among the best in her field in the Midwest. Angie uses her knowledge and personal experiences as a mother of nine to lead her clients along the path to wellness. She believes the entire person is important and refuses to work with people in pieces, because she knows that if the journey is not balanced, the life will manifest chaos.

Even though Angie has a degree as a Doctor of Natural Health, she does not diagnose or prescribe. She has become weary of people wanting to know what is "wrong" with them. She doesn't want people to focus on what's wrong. Angie knows that if you focus on what's right, you'll discover how to change what's "wrong. Angie has learned that focusing on wellness—doing all the things that one should be doing—is the answer to attracting wellness.

Angie works with individuals, couples, and groups who are ready to make necessary changes to live IN wellness daily. She instills in them that nothing is impossible and everything worth having requires action.

Make it Simple - Live in Wellness Daily

Angela Taylor

Did you know that you don't have to be perfectly fit to live IN wellness daily?

Did you know that living IN wellness daily requires that you feed your mind positive information, your body nourishing foods, and your spirit soul food?

Did you know that when you are doing all of these all at once, you are living IN wellness daily?

Our world has done a great job of complicating life, and especially complicating wellness. I choose to use the word wellness instead of health because many of us equate health with having no doctor's appointments, symptoms, diagnoses, or prescription drugs. Wellness is not about any of those things at all. AND you can choose to start living IN wellness RIGHT NOW. You don't have to wait for tomorrow, or Monday! I am going to give you some things to work on that will help you as you travel the path of wellness.

The first area of wellness we'll talk about is the mind. It is important to feed the mind positive information. This translates into how you are affected both emotionally and mentally by what you read and the discussions and interactions you have with others. It is vital to wellness that you guard your mind. Do all you can to keep the bad out. Protect your thoughts by only allowing good things to rest there. When you realize that you are speaking poorly to yourself, STOP in that instant and change the words you hear. LOVE YOURSELF in a way that only you can. There are only two people who know everything about you—you and Heavenly Father. I can testify that He is not the one who keeps throwing your faults into your face. He loves you regardless of how you have lived your life to this point and He greatly desires that YOU love you as much as HE loves you.

With all the technology around us, we have information coming at us all the time. Computers, tablets, cell phones, MP3 players, etc. that bring every form of media right into our homes and our hands. There are multiple forms of social media that are supposed to help keep us better connected with our family and friends, however, they have become a source of negativity for far too many. You may discover that you have to thin out your "Friends" list to only those who know you well OR to only those who post positive things. The more you surround yourself with positive and uplifting people, books, and music, the sooner you'll discover how wonderful life really can be.

It also might be necessary to make changes to your in-person relationships. Far too many of us are tolerating toxic people simply because we've known them all our lives or they are part of the family. Limiting your time with them doesn't have to mean telling them that they are creating negative chaos in your life unless you are ready to have that conversation. It does mean that you may need to turn down social activities of which they will also take part. None of us can afford to waste time or energy on toxic people. We can't help them. Only they can help them. Gift them a good personal improvement book (like this one) and pray that they read it. It's really the only thing you can do for them.

Now, let's talk about those people you love being around but who are, at times, verbally abusive in a joking way. Abuse is abuse and to allow it in any form is harmful to your wellness. Many people don't realize they are harming anyone. They are just having fun. I used to joke sarcastically with people until a sweet friend told me exactly how it made her feel. I hadn't realized how harmful it was and then realized that I'd grown up with and hated it when it was done to me, so what right did I have to do it to others. It's something I've stopped doing.

When we do these things to others we are desensitizing them from this form of abuse. So, if you know someone who puts on a smile and tolerates verbal abuse, have you played a role in the desensitization of their mind? If so, go apologize and ask them to tell you when you are doing it so you can make a change for the better and then take a stand whenever you see it being done to them. This helps them know you are serious about wanting to rid your life of this behavior. It also helps them find their voice and gives them the courage to stand up for themselves.

Now, let's talk about the body. The body speaks to us in both very subtle and very obvious ways. It just depends upon what it needs us to know at the time. The symptoms that we've been taught to turn off by using man-made chemical drugs are actually part of the body's communication system. Do you clip the wire when your car's fuel light comes on? OF COURSE NOT! You respond to the signal in the appropriate way by filling it with fuel. So why do we shut off the body's communication signals? The simple answer is because most people are not aware that that's what they are doing every time they swallow a pill or liquid. Living IN wellness daily is, in fact, one way that we stop and fill the body with its fuel. When the body has what it needs, it can repair itself. Don't you wish your car could do that?

NO, this does not mean that if you are currently taking man-made chemical drugs that you need to stop taking them right now. This means that you need to keep your care provider informed about the changes you are making and the desire to live IN wellness daily. Your care provider will then be able to monitor how well you are doing on this path to wellness and help you make adjustments when necessary.

When it comes to taking care of the body, we must understand that what we've been taught about fueling the body when we are overweight doesn't work. Yes, I'm talking about dieting. Dieting does not work. Dieting is part of the problem. It is not the solution. There is actually quite a bit of science emerging to back me up. Another thing to understand about fueling the body regardless of weight is that there are no foods that are truly bad for you. YES, you read that correctly. Even enjoying a slice of cake can be good for you. The key word in that sentence is "enjoying"....I'll explain in a minute what I'm talking about so for now, keep reading.

You see, you were born an intuitive eater. You were born knowing exactly how to eat, how much to eat, and when to stop eating. At some point something happened that buried that intuitive eater alive. It's time to dig your intuitive eater back out. Here are 10 things you need to know in order to live IN wellness daily as you nourish your body.

1. It's time to REJECT the dieting mentality. It's not natural to conform to eating rules. They do more harm than good. Rejecting the dieting mentality means that you get rid of all the dieting tools. Now is the time to throw out all the dieting books and articles that have promised you quick, easy, and permanent results. It's time to get angry about the lies you've been told that have led you to believe that you are a failure every time you've stopped dieting and regained all the weight (and more). If you allow even one tiny glimmer of hope that there is a diet out there that will work for you to survive, then you will keep your intuitive eater buried alive. It's also time to walk away from the scale. The scale is not your friend and isn't telling you the entire truth.

2. If you're hungry, HONOR your hunger by eating. A feeling of hunger is one of the many signs your body gives you that it needs fuel. Fuel is required for optimal performance. Your body can't

go the distance if there's not enough fuel. If there's not enough fuel, it must begin to slow down and even shut off some processes. Telling yourself "No" will only set off a primal drive to overeat by a body that thinks it's being starved. Excessive hunger is the enemy and will send a sense of panic throughout your body. Learn to honor your hunger and learn about all the different ways your body signals you for fuel. Honoring your hunger will help you relearn how to trust yourself and food.

3. Food is not the enemy, so it's time to MAKE PEACE with food. Food is vital for your survival. The body's #1 goal is to survive. Food is fuel and is what the body uses as its energy source. Give yourself unconditional permission to eat. Yes, that means to eat ANYTHING. Telling yourself that you "cannot" or "should not" have a certain kind of food will lead to intense feelings of deprivation that eventually lead to uncontrollable cravings and often times binging. (True and properly diagnosed food sensitivities and/or allergies should absolutely be respected.) Making peace with food can be the scariest part of digging out your intuitive eater. This part is about learning to trust yourself with food. It's also about learning to trust that the body knows what it's doing. The body really does know what it's doing, I promise.

4. You've spent a lifetime hearing all sorts of rules when it comes to eating. It's perfectly okay to CHALLENGE the food police. Don't allow anyone, even yourself, to control what you eat, how much you eat, how often you eat, etc. The food police monitor the crazy dieting rules you've learned over the years and attempt to keep you "compliant" with each and every one of them. It's not natural to have food rules, so they have no place in your life. Telling the food police to go away is vital to properly nourishing your body.

5. Respond to the body's satisfaction signals by RESPECTING your fullness. How does the food taste? How satisfied are you feeling? Etc…In the beginning of this process you may find that you feel as though you can't stop eating because you are afraid that the food might not be there the next time you want to eat. This is normal. Make sure that you keep food in the house; all kinds of foods. Nothing is off limits (unless you have a properly diagnosed food sensitivity or allergy). Even play foods—you know them as "junk foods"—are allowed to be in your home. Knowing they are there if you want them allows your internal voice to find peace instead of throwing a tantrum because it's been told that it can't have those kinds of foods.

6. DISCOVER the satisfaction factor when you rediscover how satisfying food can be. Did you know that the Japanese promote pleasure as one of the goals of healthy living? There is supposed to be great pleasure and satisfaction found in the eating experience. Enjoying what you are eating will aid in helping you feel satisfied and content. This is where the cake fits in. Eat it only if you can ENJOY eating it. Give yourself permission and then enjoy every single bite. When you do this for yourself, you will find that it takes far less food to feel satisfied.

7. You are an emotional creature. Learn how to HONOR your feelings without using food. There are a lot of ways to comfort, nurture, distract, and resolve emotional issues without using food. Each emotion has its own trigger and its own release. Food will not fix any of the emotional states we experience throughout the day, week, month, or year. Food will not solve the problem. Emotional eating brings with it additional negative emotions that will leave you feeling worse. We all ultimately have to learn how to deal with the source of the emotion. Often times what we are feeling is linked to a lack of self-care.

8. Accept where you are right now by RESPECTING your body. We are all different sizes on purpose. Find joy in YOUR body so you can feel better about who you are. Rejecting the dieting mentality is challenging when you are unrealistic and overly critical about your body shape. Even models have someone touching up their photos for the magazine. Buy and wear clothes that fit your body. If you can't accept you where you are right now, then how will you be able to accept you at a smaller size?

9. Forget hours of exhausting exercise! I don't even like using the word 'exercise' because it's become a negative word to me and to many of the people with whom I work. Instead, we use the word MOVEMENT because we all just need to get moving so we feel how different it is. Take calorie burning out of the equation and just enjoy moving your body. If your only goal is to lose weight, it may not be enough to motivate you to move. Then, there's the question of what's going to keep you moving once you've reached your goal? However, if your goal is to live IN wellness daily, you are more likely to continue moving throughout the day even after your body has normalized its weight.

10. Make food choices throughout the day that HONOR your health and taste buds while making you feel well. Eating a perfect diet is not required in order to live IN wellness. It is what you eat consistently over time that matters. Progress is the goal, not perfection. It may take a person years before they reach a point of being ready to consume mostly nutritious foods. This is because each person must first find peace with the comfort foods that may fall outside of the "healthy" definition. Again, this is not about eating only perfectly healthy foods all the time. It is about eating healthy foods most of the time.

By allowing these 10 things to become part of your life, you will discover a deeper understanding of nourishing the body.

The last area of wellness to talk about here is to feed your spirit soul food. Exactly what that means is different for each person. Some will find that they are spiritually lifted and fed by taking a quiet walk alone in the morning as the world is waking up. Others will find their soul food inside a book or the Holy Scriptures. Many others will find their soul food in their relationships and conversations. The biggest point that needs to be made here is that we ARE spirits living a human experience.

I've discovered in my own life that the spiritual greatly impacts and permeates every other aspect of life. The person who thinks that nurturing the spirit means only going to church on their Sabbath day is missing the point entirely. You see, YOU are an individual of great worth. You have a divine nature that has most likely not been realized nor properly used. Your divine nature is part of your purpose and reason for being here at this moment in history. YOU MATTER. Your spirit has the ability to feed and nourish others in wonderful ways.

Your spirit can lighten a room and brighten the hearts of everyone you meet. When your spirit is not properly fed, it becomes dim. It never goes out, but it is left wondering what this existence is all about. Making time each day to feed soul food to your spirit will help you live IN wellness. The spirit is part of the complete picture. Include it and experience a level of wellness you might not have ever known before.

One of the worst things we do to ourselves is being worldly. As spirits having a human experience, we must learn how to live IN the world without becoming a person OF the world. How is that done? Again, this is different for each person. Some will find that volunteering at a local shelter or food bank helps them to remember what is important in life. Others will only need to look upon their children to remember. The bottom line is this: if your life has become so complicated that you don't know which end is up and you spend more time in your car than you do enjoying good relationships and conversations, then STOP and MAKE IT SIMPLE.

Live IN wellness daily OR live IN sickness daily. It's your choice. No one can make this choice for you. I can't eat well and move more and have it impact your level of wellness. That's not how it works. All you have to do is decide. Go ahead, make a choice. CHOOSE to live IN wellness or to live IN sickness, understanding that if you choose sickness, you only have yourself to blame. You do not have the right to blame your skinny neighbor, *The Biggest Loser* television show, or the person body shaming others in their blog.

If you choose to live IN wellness, it won't be easy, but it WILL be worth it. It will mean changing in both small and big ways. If you choose to live IN wellness, you'll get to figure out what type of movement you enjoy, how to enjoy eating again, and what it feels like to be spiritually fed.

Choose to live IN wellness!

***

To contact Angie:

www.AttractingWellness.com

angie@attractingwellness.com

Twitter: @taylorangie

Facebook: www.Facebook.com/AttractingWellness

Art Costello

Art Costello lives in Austin, Texas with his wife, Beverly, and their dog, Hazel. His family includes three adult children, their spouses, and five grandchildren. His background includes serving in Vietnam as a Marine, playing college and semi-professional baseball as a catcher, working in and completing a degree in psychology, being a new talent scout in the entertainment business, and owning a business for thirty years.

Throughout it all, he has always put others before himself. The most admirable quality that is not often seen. He also puts people immediately at ease as he talks to them by asking a few questions and will almost always find a common ground on which to base a relationship. Frequently, he can determine the root of a situation you may not even understand exists after asking a question or two and will shine a light on it from a different perspective.

One thing for sure about Art is his ability to think differently. His eyes seem to look at subjects from a point of view that most cannot see until it is pointed out. He has the ability to tenderly talk to people about important subjects, yet does not cause feelings of judgments or shame. It is this quality that seems to touch the hearts of those around him the most.

What's Possible

By Art Costello

Expectation Therapy is a powerful new approach to coaching that allows individuals to reach their fullest potential. It is based on the premise that setting high expectations can unlock incredible reservoirs of inner strength, mental energy, and creativity. It is a method that helps people overcome psychological barriers and the habits that inhibit success. It is a technique that allows clients to thrive.

As a therapist or life coach, what high expectations do you set for your practice? I'm sure you want to see your clients blossoming. For instance, do you visualize them transforming their lives and coming to your sessions filled with excitement and enthusiasm because they are starting to achieve their goals? Can you imagine your clients spreading the word that you have helped them flourish more than they could have hoped for? Can you picture how fulfilling it would feel to know how vital your input and services are to the lives of the people you serve? Just envisage the joy and satisfaction you will feel knowing the positive difference you are making to others.

This is the opportunity Expectation Therapy affords you! It provides a whole new framework for thinking, one that will provide clarity and direction not only in your practice, but also your personal and family life.

How do I know Expectation Therapy can deliver results like this? Because I have lived it!!! Let me take you on the journey, which I believe can enrich your life too!

When I was nine years old, I was ripped and torn from everything that was near and dear to me. Baseball!! It's where I found my identity and purpose at a young age. My family moved from suburban New Jersey to a very remote rural little town in upstate New York. There were no kids living close enough to play ball with, and no fields where we could run and slide—just a tall mountain, overlooking a dilapidated house that was filthy dirty and virtually unlivable. It was a place that I was supposed to call home and where I should have felt safe and secure.

Instead, I felt lost and abandoned. In search of some consolation, I ventured up that mountain, struggling to make it to the top. Step by step, I moved forward in search of a spot that I prayed would bring comfort and solace to my life. Tired and sweaty, I nonetheless reached the summit. I immediately lay on my back in the tall grass while a gentle breeze blew over my little body. Then, I stared at the blue sky wondering what was to become of me, what would my life be like in the future?

I began thinking about what was happening in my life, which was so very different than it had ever been before. I had thoughts about my dad who was then hospitalized with a ruptured ulcer. Maybe his condition stemmed from the stress of the move? The strain of illness weighed on all of us. The doctors kept telling my mom they were not sure he would pull through.

Lying there on my back, I started a conversation with God. Speaking and asking the universe what was going to become of me. I heard a voice speak to me in a way I had never experienced before. It told me that everything would be okay and that if I remained faithful, then my path and calling would come.

It was then and there that I came to the realization that things had to change. I needed to take control of my life. I had to chart my destiny and carve out my future. If I did, then the feeling of security, certainty, and being loved would return.

The Change[9]

I made many journeys to my mountaintop retreat over the ensuing years. I formed a plan to escape my circumstances. At the age of 17, I made the decision to join the United States Marines. On July 21, 1965, I left that small little town and all of its memories behind. I will always remember looking out the back window of that car full of future Marines. I remember saying out loud, "Goodbye Avoca, I'll never see you again." In retrospect, I was turning off the switch on a horrible past by speaking those words. It must have been cathartic because all the others in the car were cheering right along with me.

Life in the Marines transformed me from a boy into a man very rapidly. Soon, I was in Vietnam and uncertainty reigned again in my life. But this time, I was prepared. What I wasn't prepared for was the chance meeting of this little girl! (Picture of Youn)

Let me explain how our paths crossed. I was on a short-range patrol one night that was thankfully uneventful. We were heading back to our compound through a nearby village. As dawn was breaking, I came around the side of this building, which was ostensibly an orphanage, but it was more like a shanty hut covered with grass. Through a wired fence, my eyes caught the eyes of a young girl who was staring back at me. A feeling hit me like a cannon, a blast! This little girl needed me, and I was going to do something to help her. When we got back to our base, our Chaplin was there. I asked him if we could arrange to have the orphans over for Thanksgiving dinner. He thought this was a great idea, so he arranged for the children to visit for the holiday. The children arrived at our compound and low and behold, my little Youn found me immediately and ran into my arms! This little girl changed my life forever!

In an instant, I learned a valuable life lesson: namely, that the world didn't revolve around a fellow named Art Costello. I came to realize that that I had been so self-centered, and that there was so much more to life. Too often, all I thought about was ME, ME, ME! Previously, I had thought I was the most important person in the universe. Oh, how wrong I was. And I found out why in Youn! Helping others brings incredible internal rewards while adding meaning and purpose to our lives. When we serve and care for others, we develop compassion, find worth, and discover our humanity.

Youn changed my expectations. She also filled my life with love and fulfillment, which I had longed for on that mountaintop years before (when I was about the same age as Youn!) Life is a miracle and a work in progress; we must open up ourselves to living fully!

Let's move forward in time. After leaving the Marines, I started and owned my own business. I kept using the techniques I created and developed from my past to solve problems and find solutions to living the life that I desired. Expectations are the seed from which we grow and develop. When we learn how to master our expectations and view them as a learning tool, then everything becomes clearer and more manageable. In turn, this creates a pathway towards fulfilling our desires and needs.

Of course, we all know that life never entirely goes according to our plans. For instance, in 2003, my wife of 33 years was diagnosed with ovarian cancer. After three years of a heroic battle, she passed away on Sept 16, 2006. It was a tremendous blow to our family and me. Several weeks before she died, she asked me to sit down. She wanted to tell me something that was very important to her. "You have been so good to me over the years, and I want you to know that," she said. Then she added, "I want to release you from your marriage vows so that you can find someone who needs and loves you as much as you have needed and loved me." At the time, I didn't want to believe that, so I put it aside and just listened to her. I now know what a tremendous gift she gave me. I can hardly imagine the strength of character it must have taken to say those words, but she did!

There were many dark and lonely days after she passed. However, after three years of being alone, and acting in some not so appropriate ways, I got tired of living the life I was living and had the realization that I needed to move forward. I had been in a desolate place before, but I had survived, and even gone on to thrive! So, I revisited and re-applied the lessons I learned as a nine-year-old little boy who had felt abandoned and scared. As before, I got down on my knees and asked God and the universe for the answer. One again, I heard that same voice from within saying be faithful and your potential will be fulfilled.

After 51 years of believing in that voice, I was rejuvenated and ready to start living again.

Here's where it gets really interesting and exciting! I joined several dating sites and met some, well let's say some attractive ladies, but I was disillusioned pretty quickly and still not happy, but I kept moving forward in my quest. Late one evening, I was looking around a site, and I ran across a picture of a very special lady. Her eyes caught me much like little Youn's did, so I wrote her, and we started corresponding. A month later, I wrote the following words to her: "Love your smile, let's have dinner and see if there's a spark, could be a fire." Well, the rest is history and on October 16, 2010 (marriage picture) my prayers were answered, and a promise was fulfilled.

Expectation Therapy has grown out my experience of how life events are manifested. We must soul search, clarify our expectations, and actively visualize the success and goals we aspire to.

It comes back to simplicity, a heartfelt dialogue with a higher power, and an abiding faith that we can better circumstances if we believe in ourselves. I have realized that we complicate life way too much. Life can be simplified and lived that way. I have learned that if we identify what we need to change, then we can clarify our intentions. When we solidify it in our minds and actions, then it will manifest itself in our lives.

Here's the conundrum: The what if's of life

Too many people ask: *What if I do something, and I fail? What if someone doesn't like it?* There are millions of excuses for not doing something. Remember this, there are also a million rewards for those who choose to do something.

Here's a quick story about a 20-year-old young lady, we'll call her Annie, whom I worked with. She had found herself in a very bad situation and was trying to make decisions for herself. Single and pregnant, she contacted me, seeking to find some resolution. The father of the baby wanted her to get an abortion, but she was conflicted about what to do and wanted my help. The father was abusive to her on many occasions, culminating in her seeking a restraining order against him. Using the Expectation Therapy model, I coached her towards developing clear goals and aspirations. Consequently, she acquired the confidence to work out a plan that put her on a much more wholesome and satisfying path. She has since had her child and is living in another state. Now she is creating a very productive and fruitful life on her terms!!

Let's look at Sandy's case. She is a lady in her 50's. She is well educated and works in a position of great responsibility. She also has two children and a husband. She had married at a young age to a man 20 years older than her. Over the years, he had become very controlling. He stifled her spirit and sucked the life and energy out of her. She came seeking help to save her marriage, but her husband refused any outside intervention! Using the Expectation Therapy model, I helped her identify her needs, wants, and desires so that she could be certain that she was making the best choices for herself and her children. Once she was clear and sure on what she needed, she was able to develop a plan to achieve her goals. She is now living her life by her design. Though it meant divorcing her controlling husband, she now has the life she wants with her children.

Every day, we are bombarded with negative expectations. Some are outright blatant, and some are very subtle and difficult to identify or discern. I'm sure you've heard the remarks about your expectations not mattering. Expectations are getting a bad rap. Some insist it's better not to have them at all!

Quotes:

> 1) William Shakespeare — "Expectation is the root of all heartache."
>
> 2) Cut your expectations short, lest you wallow in disappointments. But take the time to differentiate between dreams and expectations or drown in sorrowful displeasure.
>
> 3) "Blessed is he who expects nothing, for he shall never be disappointed." – Alexander Pope

In reality, expectations are the root of success. Here's what you can learn from Expectation Therapy:

- Expectations seed Independent thinking: It all starts with an Expectation!!
- Discover how to banish fear and face the unexpected with faith so that you can **start achieving your highest dreams** and living your life on your terms.
- Improve your interaction with others so that you can effectively communicate your wants, needs, and desires to achieve the results you desire.

- Learn how to **create priorities** that help you achieve what you desire, faster. This leads you to increased direction and goals, resulting in the life that you desire.
- Learn how to face unexpected changes gracefully. We all have unexpected events in life. What separates life's victories from its victims is the ability to control one's emotions. When you learn self-mastery, then you can respond to events and steer your life in the direction of your aspirations.
- Overcome grief and despair over personal losses. Again, having a pre-planned course of action will take the stress of these types of events away and bring a calm peacefulness into your life.

Sometimes, I think about that nine-year-old boy at the top of that hill so many years ago. I wonder myself, what would my life be like today had I not met Youn? What if I had I not gone through all of the things that I have gone through and learned the three steps of Expectation Therapy? Where would my life be?

You know, the reality is that I would probably be stuck in that small town in upstate New York. I probably would be trapped in a nowhere job and maybe unemployed, maybe even an alcoholic. My life would probably be going nowhere, and I probably would not have been able to serve my country! I probably would not have much value or purpose to my life! I'd be like so many people who get stuck in the ruts of life because they don't know how to step out of it.

So, what about you? What about your life? Think about where you are going to be six months from now, or a year from now, or five years from now if you keep doing the things you have always done. If you keep letting circumstances define your life, or if you keep defining your life according to somebody else's values or designs. Where are you going to be?

The Change[9]

Are you still going to be stuck in a job that you don't like and that doesn't serve you? Are you still going to be underachieving? Are you still going to struggling in your relationships with friends and family? Are you still going to be living in a place or a town or an environment that holds you back, having your dreams and goals unidentified or unrealized?

You know it happens to so many people, but think about this for a second: what happens if you do follow the steps we talked about today? What is in store for you in the next year, the next five years, if you take all three steps of Expectation Therapy and start realizing them and practicing them faithfully today? Chances are you are going to be less stressed in your life. You are likely to have a greater vision for your life, loftier goals, and an increased feeling of clarity regarding your purpose. In all probability, you will have a greater peace of mind because you'll be living life according to your values and your design. You will become the architect of your future for a change. That's what is in store for people who follow the Expectation Therapy model.

To get you started, let me challenge you with this. I encourage you to take the first step towards Expectation Therapy. The first stage is to identify. So, I challenge you in the next twenty-four hours to find a place—it could be in your office, your car, your home, or backyard (or anywhere you are comfortable)—where you can be still for twenty minutes. In that time, I want you to close your eyes and reflect deeply on how you want your life to be! Identify one thing—start with just one thing!—that is going to improve your life. Identify it, get clear on it, focus on it, visualize it, and turn that switch on so that you know exactly what it is you are working towards.

I see this as a huge opportunity for you to take your life to new levels of fulfillment and prosperity. Your will discover increased focus and resourcefulness, which will benefit your personal, familial, and professional life. Dare to set high expectations and join with me in this revolution to transform only your life, but also the world itself.

***

To Contact Art:

Expectation Therapy

Art Costello

P.O. Box 200146

Austin, TX 78759

512-996-9411

art@expectationtherapy.com

https://expectationtherapy.com

http://artcostello.com

https://www.facebook.com/ExpectationTherapy?ref=hl

https://twitter.com/myexpectation

Cheril Goodrich

Cheril is an OMC-CMT-CHT-NLP, and has studied Living Frequency. She is clear audient, an empath, has dabbled in astrology, numerology, and also has insight into understanding the symbolic meaning behind dreams.

About 20 years ago, she learned how to ask questions that would gain a response from a much Higher Invisible Source than she was accustomed to hearing. The Words that were shared with her did not come from a language she did not understand. However, the value of the Words being spoken were quite different. Because of this, it was like learning a whole new Language.

Over the next 25 years, she began to hear of a specific Universal Plan called One Wholeness Now. This Plan is a global Plan designed to undo disease, hunger, limits, old age, and even death through the specific application of miracles. This is the information she now shares.

Because miracles do not have physical words that can define what they are for, learning to speak the same Language as Miracles is her passion, and also the goal she has chosen to share with others.

On the 8th Day

By Cheril Goodrich

The Super Blood Moon on September 27, 2015 indicates that the end of days foretold in the Bible is complete. Unlike religious dogma theology often teaches, the world did not come to an end, and there was no mass destruction. Instead, something else occurred that denies scientific understanding or explanation. This is a simple interpretation, but it is not easy to grasp or understand.

We have entered a time zone of new creative potential. With this, the linear time zone with the past in tow has ended; but there is a lot of past floating around in time that has to be cleaned up. This cleanup process will take around a thousand years.

Ending time as our world understands it will not be easy. However, this transition is necessary to undo all past associations to a global deception that began thousands of years ago.

Because in reality, there are no gaps in truth; there will be no perceived loss of time. However, there will be perceived losses in personal value. Shifts in personal value are necessary for internal correction purposes. The Universal Plan designed to help individuals make value corrections is called One Wholeness Now, or OWN.

During this transition period in time, individuals will be expected to recognize the link between personal value and emotional trauma. Whether it is physical or psychological, personal trauma binds us to the past. Because all personal trauma is contaminating emotional virtue, and all personal understanding of value comes from how we emotionally experienced trauma in the past, individuals will be expected to examine how they understand their personal reality. This is because it is impossible to establish reality on the back of personal trauma. The Plan is devised to help us discover personal past traumatic blocks that are personally stored in the body as a valued memory.

The new time zone we are entering is called Virtual Time. The understanding our world uses to understand Virtual Time is invalid, as it is artificially governed. Any time zone that is artificially governed lacks the emotional substance or virtue to assist in higher u.

All value that limits the Self is deceptive value. All value that stems from the deception comes from past trauma. As individuals, it is our response-ability to find the emotionally value-less memories that are blocking our unlimited potential. This will require us to individually seek to correct the emotional body trauma that keeps us linked to the past.

Linear time, which our world has lived in for thousands of years, has come to an end. By agreeing to undo our traumatic and fearful emotional ties to the past, we will have access to a much higher degree of emotional intelligence. This is the new understanding we will carry into Virtual Time. As long as we hang on to fearful associations with the past, this is how long we will be stuck in linear time.

Linear time only allows us access to 10% of the Universal understanding that is available to us. Trauma has kept us locked into this 10%. Imagine what would happen if we only raised this percentage by 15%. This is what we are being offered. One of the problems is our paper identity.

The paper identity we were given at birth attaches us to linear time. Our true identity comes from Living Value, not paper. The dependency on paper has redefined our Living Identity by placing us in bondage to the paper laws, contracts, and death certificates.

The Change[9]

The paper that determines our reality is not stable enough to build a global foundation on. This fact is becoming more apparent.

Virtual Time, which is also called the Promised Land in the Bible, is not contaminated by paper value. Because Virtual Time is clean of all emotional contaminants or false value that were traumatically introduced, it is essential that our paper identity be purified of the past. Because our reality is defined in 3D, just eliminating the body would bring on more fear. This is not what correction is for.

It is time to recognize that paper value cannot assign any value to our Living Identity. Paper cannot fill in emotional gaps. This is impossible. Undoing the false value that has led to all of the paper deceptions in time is essential to recognize our Living or Virtual Identity.

There is a story behind the linear identity that began thousands of years ago. This story has to do with the Inno-Sense that occupied the Garden in the beginning. Inno-Sense is the start of a Living Identity. The Living Identity flows over a long period of time, which moves into seasons. Once a whole season of Inno-Sense is complete, conscious maturity is attainted.

In the beginning, Inno-Sense was deceived into believing a lie. This lie reversed the natural order reaching conscious maturity. They were told that they would be godlike if they accepted a personal identity instead of the Living One they had been given. Quite the opposite occurred.

Instead of the godlike understanding they were deceived into accepting, they were left virtually homeless in a time they were not ready to live in.

In the beginning, before the linear time line began, there were Guardians that watched over Inno-Sense. These Guardians did not have access to the same Rights that Inno-Sense did. This hardly seemed fair to the Guardians, and so they began to dote on an evil plan to tempt Inno-Sense into relinquishing their Living Rights. If Inno-Sense agreed to the deception, these Living Rights would be relinquished to the guardians. Without their Living Rights, Inno-Sense would be left unprotected and would be left to be controlled by the guardians. Thus, guardians would become masters of Inno-Sense. By becoming masters of Inno-Sense, they could manipulate the Living Flow in Virtual Time.

This evil plan was discovered immediately before Living Flow was contaminated, but not before Inno-Sense was violated.

It is important to note that Guardians do not actively play an active role in Time. The evil plan was an attempt to place them in a position of actively participating in Time. If this occurred, they too would have access to the Living Truth that flows through time. Catching the deception immediately prevented Virtual Time from being contaminated, but Inno-Sense had already been contaminated. Thus, they were bound to linear time where the lie was contained. The end of days signals the end of the violation of Inno-Sense.

Because Inno-Sense now shared the same linear time as the deception, civilizations would continue to follow the deception as well. But there has always been a Plan in effect that would undo the error that Inno-Sense had made, while bringing eventual justice to the evil guardians.

This deception was obviously a Universal conspiracy, or an attempt to undermine the Living Laws that govern the Living Identity. Fortunately, this conspiracy was caught immediately, and a Plan was set into motion to undo all of this innocent nonsense. However, a whole collective Living Identity had been contaminated. In order to purify Inno-Sense, generations of individuals would march through linear time until the end of days was complete.

The violation of Inno-Sense split the One Whole Sense of Now, or Virtual Time, into five separate body senses. When Inno-Sense was tricked into accepting an identity separate from the Whole Collective Living Body defined by whole truth, the individual body identity split into five separate body senses. In between each of the five body senses is a tiny gap where a non-sense was formed out of the darkness of the lie. This gap between the senses is called fear. It is within this fearful gap that all guilt in linear time is upheld. There is no gap in Virtual Time because there is no gap in Living Truth. This gap exists in us, or the paper body identity, not reality. Only in a gap could a paper identity, along with a paper society, be used to govern a whole world.

Linear time is littered and contaminated with guilt. This guilt cannot be seen, but it can be felt in the body. The body detection of guilt does not intrude in Virtual Time. This is because all guilt is assigned to a past reference in linear time.

The way we personally deal with guilt is generally by attempting to hide it. By hiding guilt, we promote and protect our paper identity. Anything we attempt to hide is an attempt to hide from truth. Only the truth will set our Inno-Sense free, and us as well.

Body fear makes no sense, so it is a non-sense. Within this gap of non-sense, a world emerged where a separate identity could be maintained on a linear time line until the end of days. The linear time line runs from birth, to life, and then into death. The time line that we will journey on will move from birth, into life, and then into rebirth. The rebirthing process will move our paper body identity into a Collective Whole Living Identity. This will not end the body, but it will redefine its purpose. A body without a deceptive past will have a whole new purpose. This will change everything we have learned to believe is possible. It will in fact shift the Law of Cause and Effect.

The End of the Inno-Sense means that we have entered The Coming of Age. Most people know that we are being lied to. Whereas innocence is as trusting as it ever was, as mature adults we are ready to end the lies of false promises. The Universal Plan of One Wholeness Now will provide us the means

Reclaiming Virtual History

As a global society, we have grown up, but we have lost major pieces of our true historical value. This truth is necessary to end the deception, and begin putting a whole collective sensory world together again. A Virtual Picture of historical truth must be established to undo the deceptive paper value that we have allowed to be assigned to our world. Until we can bear witness to the truth, the deception will continue to intrude on our collective efforts to restore Living Flow in our world.

The Plan of OWN has been in effect for thousands of years. Although it is not our response-ability to undo the deception, as the Plan will deal with this, it is our responsibility to map out the paper identity that lives on the fragmented linear time line. The means to separate what is real from what is a lie is being provided. This Living Tool that works in linear time to sort out this mess and correct the error is called a miracle.

Miracles undo guilt in time by denying the existence of any guilt in linear time that began in the body as a trauma. Trauma disrupts natural flow in time. Once this occurs, guilt moves in. This guilt establishes a link to body fear. In effect, guilt and fear live off of each other. The miracle stands in time between the middle of body fear and guilt. We are being asked to learn how to exchange body fear for a miracle. This will completely dissolve the deceptive link that exists between the two, and thus restore a whole collective emotional link to the natural flow in Virtual Time.

Allow me please to give you an example of how this works.

For many years, I was a practicing massage therapist. During this time, I began to explore the mind/body connection and how the mind communicated with the body. This exploration taught me that there was a form of communication going on between the mind and the body that most people do not even realize is there. In the beginning, muscle pain became the focus of my exploration, as massage therapy deals with muscles.

The first time this became evident to me was when a woman came in complaining about a pain in her back. I asked her how long she had the pain, to which she replied four months. She then said something interesting. She said that she had not experienced this pain in 20 years. I then asked her what happened four months ago, to which she replied, her mother had died. This was all very interesting to me, as I had never associated body pain with emotional pain. I just thought it was physical pain. As I explored further, I began to look at the fear involved in emotional pain.

I found myself helping individuals who would allow me to explore their physical pain that was attached to some kind of personal trauma. Of course, there was always some kind of fear attached to this trauma.

One example involved an individual who was came in for a massage. She had pain in her female organs that would not go away. The pain was so bad, she had her reproductive organs surgically removed. During her massage, I asked her if she had ever been sexually violated, at which point she began to cry.

When she was 12 years old, her uncle raped her. She never told anyone out of fear of being blamed and shamed. Fear is of the body, and guilt is in time. The memory of guilt in time kept the fear alive in the body where the pain was emanating from, but the original fear began as a result of a physical and psychological trauma.

I helped her become the conscious hero in her own linear nightmare. By showing her how to go back in time to protect her inner child from this seemingly living terror, her fear was gone. She found that she could protect her inner child, and thus end the constant fear of having to tell. I perceive the fear of being blamed and shamed for her uncle's inappropriate behavior was emotionally more devastating than the rape.

Once the body fear was gone, there was no more guilt attached to the episode. By disconnecting body fear from the guilt held in linear time, there was no more emotional attachment to the experience. With no more emotional attachment to the experience, the deceptive control over her body was gone. As peace was restored to her body, mind, and soul, this was indeed a miracle.

What I have discovered is that once body fear is exchanged for a miracle in time, something totally unexpected is revealed. Lost pieces of Virtual History are restored in the mind of the individual. I now understand this is the revelation of Living Truth that had been hiding behind the deception in linear time. As a piece of whole truth is revealed to the individual, a whole picture of a collectively defined truth emerges. This truth will be used to define a whole New World.

All body trauma teaches that we are vulnerable and fear is necessary to protect the body. This makes no sense, and is therefore a non-sense. Only whole sanity reveals truth, and truth is what the miracle delivers. The miracle offers us a new reason to hope. This hope is beyond belief, but not beyond the faith that only the individual can provide.

The Plan to access miracles to undo past emotional trauma leaves no room for exceptions. This Plan opens the door to A Season of Miracles. A Season of Miracles offers us the means to understand the global shifts that are going on.

Each miracle that happens causes a ripple effect in time. These ripples collectively restore our Virtual Emotions. Once all Virtual Emotions have been restored, the whole world will enter into Virtual Time, together. Gone will be war, injustice, crime, disease, death, hunger, and the list goes on. We the people are being asked to be part of this Miracle Revolution. This is a peaceful revolution that only miracles can provide.

Each individual has a Team of Inner Advisors and Counselors ready to assist them in making the shift from fear to a miracle. How and when the individual chooses to begin their miracle journey is up to them. However, what they will learn is not.

Because everything we have learned in linear time is contaminated with the deception, nothing has prepared us for what awaits us on this miracle journey through time. Miracles must be experienced to be appreciated, not interpreted. Although a Universal Theology is impossible, a Universal experience is not only possible, it is necessary. This is the miracle experience.

It is impossible for me to explain to you the immediate peace that is experienced during the fear to a miracle shift. I have witnessed a complete undoing of a chronic body symptom, and also witnessed a body take on a whole new physical appearance.

The Coming of Age means that we are consciously ready to receive miracles. These are the miracles that promise rebirth, not of the body—although the body is but part of the experience—but of our collective truth.

The end of days calls for a new beginning. A new beginning calls for birth, life, and then rebirth. Everything we need to begin this journey is here and now. The Plan of OWN has not left one detail out. This is a Plan that has been actively working for thousands of years, making sure we do not individually go so deeply into the deception that it would be impossible for miracles to rescue us.

Not one individual will be left behind. Everything we want, miracles have to offer us. Everything we don't want exists on a deceptive linear time line that no longer serves any purpose. It is time to begin the miracle journey across time.

To Contact Cheril:

http://themiraclealchemist.com

http://onthe8thday.com

On Facebook

https://www.facebook.com/OneWholenessNow

https://www.facebook.com/miracleresponse

https://www.facebook.com/TheGreatMiracleShare

https://www.facebook.com/themiraclealchemist

On Pinterest

https://www.pinterest.com/miracleshare/

Phone: 863-325-3128

Email: cherilsword@gmail.com

Diana Garber

A reporter once remarked in his article that Feng Shui Master Diana Garber 'isn't your typical candle-sniffing cloud watcher.' She's a change agent and her results have transformed the minds of many skeptics.

She lived a disciplined corporate life while simultaneously pursuing feng shui. As VP of a Fortune 100 company, she oversaw 65,000 workstations and 2,500 servers. She's worked command centers for the NY terrorist attack, Hurricanes Lili & Isidore, the Ft. Worth tornado, and more.

Diana thrived through 20 major surgeries, two near-death experiences, and the loss of children. She says, "manage your environment consciously or it unconsciously manages you©."

She has achieved much success in the feng shui world and has many firsts to her name: Clinical Instructor and Feng Shui practitioner for The Ohio State University; 1st U.S. integrative health center; 1st Feng Shui Master to be speak at a medical convention; 1st Certified Feng Shui practitioner for Academy of Integrative Health & Medicine; 1st U.S. Feng Shui-designed office building; 1st to receive medical referrals; and much more. Diana is an author and has been featured on ABC, CBS, FOX, and NPR.

Three Powerful Words

By Diana Garber

Who are you? Tell me about yourself. Isn't that what we want to know about another human being, or want someone to know about us? It's more meaningful than "What do you do?" or "Where do you work?" It takes me back to the early 90s, when a communications course instructor arranged a small group of us to conference with Iranians on Christmas day. Talk about intimidating! I wondered ...*What do I say? How do I start a conversation?* Now you know.

Where are you? What has been your journey? I believed Mom and Dad would have relished being asked that (to be able to tell their story). So before my parents passed, I sat with them as we went through old pictures. Instead of asking "Who are those people, where was that taken?" I asked, "This picture—what was going on in your life; what were your worries, and what were your joys?" I obtained a whole new appreciation of them. Until then, I had my story about my childhood, but it was only part of the story.

Mom was an orphan who grew up in Australia. She married Dad during WWII and while he was serving, came to America to be met by prejudice and disdain. So allow me to share a little more background as to my journey, then I'll share insights into self-empowerment by using three powerful words. Why three words? According to feng shui, I'm a three, hardwood person. For quite some time now, I wake up thinking of three-word phrases, so that's what I'm meant to share.

Dad drove truck for a while. He was gone from home a lot, leaving Mom to raise two boys while working. She was ahead of her time, but then she received a lot of criticism doing so. They agreed that if he came off the road, they would try for a daughter. Dad was close to his sister who was killed in a car accident two weeks before she was to marry. Mom said she was thrilled to have a girl (but once I was born, I didn't experience it that way). Mom was jealous as Dad and I grew very close. He called me Sis and my little hands came in handy working in the garage with him.

Mom rewarded me for cooking and cleaning, and scolded me for anything else. I'd clean all day (including eight shelves of salt and pepper shakers, which she collected), do the ironing, and have a meal ready. She'd come home after work and look around, then say, "That register is dirty." What I did was never enough.

Once she held a knife to my throat and said she wished I was gone. Little did she know she'd get her wish. In all fairness to Mom, as mentioned she grew up in an orphanage. Her mother left her there and lied about her age so no one would figure out who the father was. Mom wasn't wanted, didn't know how old she was, and didn't have a role model. Then she moved to the U.S. and was rejected here. She worked tirelessly to please everyone, and lost herself.

We lived in a basement house for my first ten years. Floods devastated our home and if it weren't for the American Red Cross, we wouldn't have had clothes to wear. Dad hunted for food and when we didn't have meat, we ate porridge for most meals that often had weevils in it. Once while hunting, Dad was shot and almost died. The man who shot him literally had coke-bottle-thick glasses and thought Dad was a squirrel. A 200-pound squirrel? He lived with the pain of buckshot in his system throughout his life.

Our entire family had health issues. Being poor, we had to make due. When colds happened, we'd grind horseradish and eat it. When my brother hemorrhaged, we learned to love liver and endive to support him. Mom was diabetic and had painful varicose veins. We foraged for herbs to make poultices. My other brother was placed in 'retarded class' because they didn't have a diagnosis back then for dyslexia. As I learned in school, I'd teach Mom and Pat. I wrote

The Change[9]

about Pat in *The Gratitude Project, a Celebration of Personal Heroes* (a collection done to honor 9/11).

Dad was a good man, but had a temper. He was working swing turn (one week of day shift, afternoon shift the next week, then a week of midnights). One night he finished the midnight shift and went to bed. I delighted at figuring out musical tunes on a broken piano we were gifted after one of the floods. Well, I woke Dad up. When he woke, he never missed his coffee and cigarettes, but this time went straight outside, hooked a chain to his truck, and dragged the piano to the backyard. He took a sledge hammer to it, then lit it on fire. That was the end of my musical career. I remember anger in our household mostly, but there were happy moments too.

We had a large garden which Pat and I tended to. Mom, Ninney (paternal Grandmother who came to live with us, always had an axe to grind with Mom, and was just a generally mean person), and I canned food for the winter. **Lemons make lemonade**. Competencies turn into skills, and now gourmet meals manifest from humble ingredients.

That's a bit of my journey, and the truth of it is I feel quite blessed. We all have heavy boots to wear. ***It's called life.*** So many of you reading this have it much worse than me. The news reminds us every day that life isn't a walk in the park. You read my bio—surgeries, death, and tragedies. Life groomed me for a career in disaster recovery and business continuity; as well as another risk management career (feng shui).

When speaking with battered women who have left their situations and are returning to the workforce, I start by saying, "I was you. ***There is hope.***" Who am I? Where am I? If I were any better, I wouldn't be walking this earth! Let me explain ...

What I've learned:

- ***Life is complicated.*** God didn't send me back once, but twice. The physical plane is the cooking pot. We're here to learn, and we seem to learn more from pain than joy. There are glimpses of joy, thankfully, and I had to cook a little more.
- ***It's our choice. Avoid victim thinking.*** As I lay there on the surgery gurney going in for a C-section, I saw the assignment board. It said, "Garber 3/0." Those were my odds to date (3 pregnancies and zero live births). Luckily, she was my first live birth. Unluckily, she never left the hospital. We don't honor those in our life (or were in our life) by blaming others or holding on to anger. Unlike my then father-in-law who said I sent her to eternal damnation because she wasn't baptized before her death (he watched Sunday morning wrestling while the family went to church), I've learned there are circumstances beyond our control. ***Create positive energy.***
- ***Mistakes make people. Do not judge.*** To the institution that required me to have the first flu vaccine (or lose my job) to show the public it was safe (I was seven months pregnant and my daughter was plagued with issues, then passed); to my abusers; to the physicians who botched surgeries; to everyone who has hurt and harmed me … ***I forgive you.*** Forgive everyone of everything.
- ***Survive or thrive.*** Surviving is being behind the eight ball (so to speak). Thriving doesn't mean there aren't hurdles, or lessons to learn; it's just a lot more invigorating.
- ***Breakdown to breakthrough.*** Think yin and yang. One doesn't exist without the other. Stuff is going to happen.
- ***Please help me.*** We get in our own way. Going it alone, and not asking for or accepting help from others is actually selfish. Don't block the flow…flow out/flow in.
- ***Balance is key.*** If you like helping but aren't willing to receive, it robs the other person of the joy of giving. Make sense?

The Change[9]

- ***Change is good.*** The birds know it, the squirrels do too. They know to plan and prepare. We as humans seem to think change is thrust upon us, when change is the only constant. **Learn from yesterday.**
- ***Plan for tomorrow.*** Yes, it is unknown, but it's better to plan and not utilize the plan, than not to plan at all. Those who don't, take from those who do. That creates conflict.
- ***Quality versus quantity.*** How many of us obsess about the one thing we didn't do or say, or the one bad comment that came back to us? ***Let it go!*** Get on with being great. Do what's right, versus what's convenient.
- ***Pursuit of happiness.*** Remember that making a living is not the same as making a life. I'm still working on this one (the family work ethic has me in its clutches). Be defined by who you love versus who loves you back.
- ***Nurture your best.*** Which describes you—pleasing the masses, or spending quality time with a few? There's freedom in being the best you can be, and if you give it all away, there may be nothing left to give. No one is in charge of your happiness but you. To be a limitless vessel of love, include yourself.
- ***Make seconds count.*** We can't change the past. It's done and over. There is only the present. Our brain takes every thought and tries to categorize it into what it knows (the past), or anticipates (the future which is unknown so based on fears or expectations). Be present in your life. ***Now or never.***
- ***Cry for commercials.*** That may sound strange, but life causes tears. Now I cry for joy. Sometimes when a commercial comes on, my husband and I just pass the tissue box because we know it will make us laugh until we cry. We've learned to like crying and to enjoy special moments that take our breath away.
- ***Emotions affect health.*** Holding on to sorrow, depression, angst, or anger is going to cost more than you can fathom. It's not worth it. Ask yourself if the pursuit of righteousness (being

Insights into Self-Empowerment

right) is worth the energy (your energy) it consumes. Be wise, not righteous.
- ***Keep the faith.*** I lost mine for a while. I was angry at God and started down a road of self-destruction, wallowing in my misery. I'm so thankful I found my way back. ***God is gratitude. Gratitude is God.***

Today's a gift:

- *Let fear go. Only hope remains.*
- *Wake your dreams.*
- *Live in possibility.*
- *Always be yourself.*
- *Speak your truth.*
- *Believe in you.*
- *Organize, simplify, transform.*
- *Music is art.*
- *Life is art. Color me up.*
- *Family is forever.*
- *Love is everything.*
- *Be in service.*
- *Set an example.*
- *Be a champion.*
- *Be a hero.*
- *Be the change.*
- *Be the light.*
- *You are loved.*

So let me state for the record, these insights are a work in progress. Some of it I have down and the rest is still evolving. My dad said it best ... when we stop learning, we're in the ground.

Please read the three-word phrases one more time, on their own. Does anything resonate with you? We all have low times, and we all have wisdom to share. What wisdom can you pay forward? Do tell (write me)!

Having fun yet?

You are blessed!

Every person counts.

You are important.

***

To Contact Diana:

http://www.IntuitiveConcepts.com

http://www.EvolveLove.net

http://www.DianaGarber.com

http://www.FengShui.Education

Diana Scanlan

Diana lives and works on Sydney's Northern Beaches on the East Coast of Australia where she operates her Natural Health and Healing Practice.

Having been blessed with the gift of Medical Intuition since childhood, she is able to see what and where your wellness challenges are and targets the healing directly to that area giving intense relief and regeneration.

She has a deep understanding of human suffering and is caring, empathetic, and non-judgemental. Diana also provides valuable information to help you through your health challenges on your journey to total wellness and freedom from pain.

Diana is a certified Life Coach, specializing in Natural Health and Wellness, and a Certified 21st Century Energy Healer. She is also a Reiki Master (Usui System of Natural Healing), has a Oneness Awakening Course Certificate of Acknowledgement, and is certified in The Secrets of Chakra Wisdom.

Professional Associations:

Associate Member International Institute of Complementary Therapies

Founding Member of Impact Coaching

Diana is the author of the forthcoming book, *Lessons From Your Last Life and How They Can Help You In This One* scheduled to be published early in 2016.

Heal Yourself, Heal the Planet

How personal change will increase planetary harmony

By Diana Scanlan

When the earth is ravaged and the animals are dying, a new tribe of people shall come unto the earth from many colours, creeds, and classes and who by their actions and deeds shall make the earth green again. They shall be known as the warriors of the rainbow.

—Hopi prophecy

The Tide has turned! And here we are shifting with our Rainbow Warrior hearts and healing to regenerate our beautiful planet.

We have been given the power to influence planetary changes in subtle but powerful ways, but first we need to heal and re-balance our own health.

We have been led to believe that if we exercise every day, eat a good healthy diet free from processed food, drink eight glasses of water every day, and enjoy seven to eight hours of good uninterrupted restful sleep, we will be happy and experience perfect health.

Having followed these guidelines, many people are saying "Hey, why aren't I feeling well?"

In today's world, we are faced with many new challenges to our wellness. Increased toxicity in our food and in the air we breathe. We are exposed to an increasing amount of E.M.F.'s (electric magnetic fields) and chemicals in our foods on a daily basis, and are overwhelmed by our workloads and family responsibilities.

Here I am focusing on the additional, lesser known contributors to vibrant health which are equally as valuable to include in our lives on a day-to-day basis.

By incorporating at least some of these into your life, you will find increased awareness, wellness, well-being, and connection with your mind, body, and spirit as well as with Universal Energy, and you will give a valuable boost to the health of our planet.

We are all aware how difficult it is to remain calm and stress free in today's hectic and often depleting working environment. A habit I adopted many years ago of finding time to spend meditating each day has helped me cope with some extreme crises which have confronted me.

I believe meditation to be one of the most powerful practices for personal change at all levels of your being. It has major benefits for physical, emotional, and spiritual health.

Regular meditation will improve your metabolism, increase ability for deep restful sleep, improve brain function, lower blood pressure, decrease tension headaches and muscle aches, reduce stress, boost your immune system, and even reduce aging!

Quite an impressive list!

Added to that the mental and emotional benefits include a decrease in anxiety levels, increased intuition, reduced perception of any problems we may have, increased happiness, peace of mind, and emotional stability.

Being in a place of serenity and calm enables this to be radiated out into your environment, ultimately bringing harmony to our planet.

Because we lead such busy lives, many people believe they have little or no time for meditation. Not so. Try this breath technique which takes only minutes and can be done at your desk or on your lunch break or, better still, walking out in nature.

Take a deep breath into your belly and as you do so, visualise peace, calm, and harmony infusing your whole being. Breathe out stress, frustration, and anger. (Insert here whatever you need to eliminate at this time.)

Repeat this technique as many times as you feel you need and enjoy your newfound serenity.

Nurture a connection with your Divine whether this is the Universe, Source, Spirit, God, Buddha, Muhammad, or any other being you feel an affinity with.

This could also be Mother Earth/Mother Nature or Nature spirits, Angels, or Guides.

Following this path on a daily basis can bring untold peace, joy, and a connection like no other.

I find that if I begin my day in quiet contemplation and gratitude even for a few minutes, the rest of the day flows easily and smoothly, even though I may encounter stress or blockages in my path.

At the end of the day, I journal the blessings and things I am thankful for, even the small and sometimes easily overlooked occurrences, a child's laughter, the perfume of roses or of newly mown grass. Awaken all your senses to the beauty and love that is all around you and which is often ignored or goes unnoticed and watch your life and well-being escalate to new levels of wonder and appreciation.

How many people have you heard saying "I hate my body, hair, teeth" or any other part of their anatomy? In their eyes they perceive themselves as being far from perfect. Whereas this is in part true—very few people have what may been seen as the perfect body. Even high-profile celebrities and models are continually striving to be "perfect."

Here we are looking at not only our outer appearance, but our inner self. We may have done something which we deeply regret and look back upon with guilt and shame. Hating ourselves for our thoughts, words, or deeds.

In addition, we may carry this guilt for years or even our whole lifetime. With this burden upon our mind and soul, total well-being and wellness will evade us and yet it can so easily be healed. We are all unconditionally loved by Source/ Spirit/ God/ the Universe or whomever you look upon as your Divine.

Only you can resolve this inner imbalance—How? By loving yourself, and looking inside yourself every day with love. Know that you are a child of the Universe and you create your world and the world around you with your thoughts.

I think back in my own life to a time when I attracted people with dark energy and intent. However, when I discovered this amazing ancient Huna technique in my life, my contacts, friendships, and life path dramatically changed to one of inner peace, harmony, and joy. Burdens were lifted and abundance in every sense of the word flooded in, and it happened virtually overnight.

If we are carrying guilt from past misdeeds, or are holding feelings of anger against those who may have hurt us, we cannot heal and move forward with our life.

I have found excellent results from Ho'oponopono. Which in essence means to make right, and is a simple step to lasting healing.

1. I love you

2. I'm sorry

3. Forgive me

4. Thank you

Ho'oponopono: Repeat these affirmations until you feel this disharmony has been reduced and resolved.

Always do this with love. Repeat to yourself or those you are not in complete harmony with "I'm sorry," "I love you," so simple—so powerful.

By forgiving others, we are essentially forgiving ourselves, which in turn can lift our guilt and heal our world. Self-forgiveness is one of the most important aspects of wellness, peace, and harmony in our lives.

"I'm sorry" and "Forgive me" are your declaration that you are not in perfect harmony with either a person, or persons, or yourself and you wish to make this right. Asking for permission to forgive not only others, but also yourself. "Thank you" signifies you are trusting the problem will be resolved for everyone's highest good. "I Love you" opens the way to recommence the movement of loving energy.

Have you noticed that if you smile at those you pass in the street, they will invariably smile back. This has the potential to not only change their day, but may ultimately change their life.

A smile will light up your face, changing your countenance with the added benefit of making you look years younger.

Similarly, laughter is a great form of internal exercise; muscles become active, respiration increases, and your facial muscles, arms, legs, and stomach get a mini workout!

If you can appreciate one level of humour called "Cosmic Humour," seeing the paradoxes and absurdities of life, a well-known doctor has said, you are likely to be more flexible and able to deal with life's ups and downs more easily.

It is a great stress reliever for tension and even pain and puts everything in perspective. In fact, some hospitals now have a laughter room, such is its healing power.

And it's impossible to overdose on it!

Grounding, or earthing, is literally connecting with the earth and feeling her energy flowing through your whole being.

Here are three wonderful practices for grounding.

Spend time in nature, walk with bare feet on the grass or sand.

Hug a tree!! Yes, without a thought of those who would ridicule this. It is wonderful to clear your energy field of E.M.F.s as well.

Have a cleansing bath using sea salt and baking soda or even better swim in salt water— the ocean is wonderful as a rejuvenating and cleansing experience.

E.M.F.'s and how they can harm your health.

In this era, we are surrounded by electrical gadgets and devices in our homes and cities, and even in the open air we are not immune and are exposed to transmitting pylons and cell phone towers.

There is mounting evidence that microwave ovens, computers, personal phones, and cordless phones are a hazard to our health and can cause headaches, cholesterol imbalances, memory malfunction, fatigue, and even cancer.

Here's how you can protect yourself:

Unplug all appliances when not in use.

Consider an organic crystal-based E.M.F. protective pendant or pyramid which is especially important if you live close to (within five kilometres) of a cell phone tower.

Mother Nature is a great diffuser of E.M.F.'s. Walk or sit with bare feet at the park, beach, or in your own garden.

Touch or even better, hug a tree. Trees have this most amazing ability if you tune to their vibration. It is possible to actually feel their energy pulsating through your being.

The Change[9]

No matter what your circumstances are, the benefits of gratitude are transformative. Over time through many personal crises, I have proved to myself just how powerful this practice is when used every day. When written in your journal, it is instilled in your subconscious mind—even when your life seems at its lowest point. If you focus on five reasons to be grateful each morning before rising and five each night before sleeping, it will boost your happiness, help with more restful sleep, and dissipate negative emotions and depression. Victim mentality is common in times of stress and hardship. "Why is this happening to me?" "Why do I not have sufficient money, friends, loving family, etc.?" (add your own feelings here). One of the best benefits of gratitude is that it helps boost your immune system, leading to greater wellness and your body's ability to fight viruses and infections.

As we grow older, or indeed at any age, we often take on a different perspective. Sometimes it can be a negative one, whereby we become resistant to change, stuck in a rut in which we find that we are unwilling to dig our way out of. Taking a life path which seems dull and depressing. Life is all about change—the seasons change, the moon waxes and wanes, the tides ebb and flow. When acceptance and a positive attitude seem out of your reach, tune into your inner being, your personal Divine, contemplate and manifest a new mindset to determine your way forward. Visualise "The Light at the End of The Tunnel" coming closer and keep striving towards it minute by minute, hour by hour, a small baby step forward each day. Remember you are supported by a Loving Universe all your life, helping, protecting, and encouraging you every step of the way. Trust in this loving energy and it will change your life.

Many years ago, I was told by my mentor at that time to be focussed, to be aware, and to be alert. Over time, I have slowly integrated these into my mind and my life on a daily basis. Why are these three strategies so important?

Focus in your life will lead you towards accomplishing your goals and following your divine life path. Insights and intuition are then received and accessed more easily. Awareness helps the movement of your day, its direction, and adjustment along the way when necessary.

Being alert to change either by choice or necessity will enable you over time to make wise decisions which will benefit yourself and those you interact with.

Worry and anxiety are basically creating future outcomes in your mind which you neither want nor need. In addition, an ongoing excess of anxiety and worry about issues which may or may not already exist will eventually create illness and disease. It is now thought that as many as sixty percent of doctor visits are directly related to anxiety, worry, and stress. A sobering thought. The following techniques are what I call, "Stress, worry, and anxiety first aid."

Tell yourself "I am doing well." "I can easily cope with all this." If you have difficulty in believing it, say it as though you do.

Pinch the web between your thumb and first finger, and breathe deeply. This is a great stress reliever.

Stand tall and breathe in through your nose while stretching your arms above your head, palms together.

As you begin breathing out through your mouth, turn your palms outward and slowly bring your arms down beside you, reaching outwards with your fingertips, whilst telling yourself "I am perfectly calm."

Try Bach Flower Rescue Remedy. It's a powerful helper in times of crisis.

I have found foot reflexology to be a great anxiety reliever. Using using a tennis ball, or better still a golf ball, in a backwards and forwards movement along your feet will stimulate the nerve endings in your sole and heel, and release tension throughout your body. Start with two minutes for each foot, each day and increase to a maximum of five minutes.

If you have a problem that just won't go away, make an appointment with it!

Each day, set aside fifteen minutes and settle down to concentrate on it. Give yourself permission to worry about it as much as you like for fifteen minutes only. Set a timer to make sure you don't overstep the time. If you begin to worry at other times, stop and tell yourself you have done all the worrying necessary for this problem.

This is my favourite—worry while you wash up or clean the floors, and throw them away with the dirty water.

Write it down along with all the awful possibilities which could eventuate, then tear up the paper into small pieces and throw them away or burn them. Finally, good news for lovers of chocolate (aren't we all)—research has found that chocolate stimulates the stress-relieving brain chemical serotonin. It is also a great source of antioxidants. However, remember to indulge in moderation and only consume the dark variety.

Try this short anxiety-relieving meditation.

Sit or lie comfortably and gently close your eyes. Visualise that you are in a quiet, peaceful garden. It is pleasantly warm and the sun is shining softly down on you. At the end of the garden is a gate. Walk through while noticing the texture of the weathered wood as you push it open. Beyond it are steps leading down to a secluded beach, with waves gently lapping on the sand. Walk slowly down, feeling the coolness of the stone steps under your feet. As you count the steps, notice that with every step you feel more relaxed and deeply calm. Your mind is open to all the good things in your life.

On this beautiful beach, you know that you are perfectly safe and can leave whenever you want. Enjoy the peace and serenity that you find here. Nearby is a seat facing the beach; walk over to it and sit down while saying to yourself, "I am peaceful, happy, and perfectly in control of my life. I cope easily with everything that happens."

You can now relax at will by remembering this peaceful place. Repeat your affirmation and add, "I can relax at will simply by thinking of this place."

When you are ready, return to the steps, knowing that you can come back here at any time you need to relax.

Count each step as you slowly return to your day.

Many people are familiar with Dr. Masaru Emoto's experiments with water, whereby he unveiled proof that our emotions and thoughts affect the structure of water, especially when sourced from pristine springs.

The water infused with happy thoughts such as "love, "peace," or "harmony" caused it to form beautiful, symmetrical, and often intricate snowflake-like images, whereas emotions such as "anger" or "hate" brought about ugly, shapeless images. Bearing in mind our bodies are composed of approximately eighty percent water and the earth fifty percent, infusing your water with love before consuming it will assist in healing your body.

This has been demonstrated in another experiment known as "The Maharishi Effect, whereby a "critical mass" of one percent of a city's population meditate together. Transcendental Meditation or calming of the mind in consciousness, the energy generated transforms the community to one of peace and increased contentment.

This meditation is so powerful that it has been proven to reduce crime by up to eighteen percent, as well as pollution and terrorism by a similar percentage in any given city.

On a wider perspective, if enough people were to participate, we could embody worldwide peace, harmony, and love. An awesome concept indeed!

A daily meditative practice by the individual can literally change your health and well-being and assist with planetary healing.

***

To contact Diana:

www.beingnaturallyhealthy.com

diana@beingnaturallyhealthy.com

Frenee Dellosa

Frenee Dellosa is a Registered Nurse by training whose specialty is Maternal Child Health. She considers Nursing to be her calling and loves her job and the people she works with. She is a bookworm who can read all day. She is also an artist, writer, and a travel enthusiast. Photography is her passion and is never without her camera when out and about. She dedicates this book to everyone who has experienced stress and conquered it.

Free your mind right now!

By Frenee Dellosa

Everyone wants peace of mind. The fast-paced world we live in makes it a challenge to attain the tranquility we so desire. Stress seems to be the common denominator that permeates our lives. Its effects are enormous. It can make us sick emotionally and physically.

Blanking your mind is one of several ways that can help you manage the stress in your life. It can be done practically anywhere. Once you feel proficient at doing it, you will be able to do it anytime you are confronted with negativity or an unexpected situation beyond your control.

Blanking your mind can give you peace of mind when practiced regularly. The benefits of attaining this much-needed peace can improve your capacity to think, enable you to make decisions that you won't regret, improve your outlook, and you make you easier to get along with.

What is peace of mind?

It is a state of being wherein one is free of fear, worries, unhappiness, unhealthy mind or body, feeling of want or hopelessness or of being unloved. Everybody wants it, but not all can attain it for one reason or other.

It has been said that without peace of mind, happiness is impossible. One can see that our fast-paced world has thrown us a lot of curveballs and it behooves the mind as to how to deal with it. Take sleeping pills, for example. Pharmaceutical companies have made huge profits from selling something that ostensibly helps people to fall asleep. Not only that, the majority of us have increasingly relied on medications to take care of our high blood pressure, headaches, and other afflictions. Add to that the need for antidepressants and psychological counseling. It seems that getting control of our lives is a real challenge.

Before anything else, we need to know ourselves. What are your core values? Do you know your own mind? What motivates you? Do you know your strengths and weaknesses? What are your beliefs? Do you love yourself? These are questions that need real and honest answers.

Loving yourself is important. How can you love others if you do not love yourself? If you love yourself, you will take good care of your physical, mental, and spiritual needs. Only then will you be able to take care of the needs of others in your circle and your fellow man as a whole.

It is a known fact that our minds are filled with constant chatter. Thoughts fill our minds no matter what. It can cloud our thinking, it can paralyze us into doing nothing if we do not take control of it. Learning to control our minds is an acquired behavior. One must learn to blank one's mind when it is confronted with negative or undesirable thoughts. We need to find a quiet place to do it. First, take slow deep breaths, close your eyes, and blank your mind of the thoughts swirling in your head. If you have not done this before, be patient with yourself. It takes practice to get rid of the constant mind talk going on in your head. Sometimes thoughts will keep intruding, but just get rid of them the best you can. Once you succeed in ridding your mind of all the clutter, keep it blank while breathing normally. After a couple of minutes, open your eyes and you are good to go. You will discover that whatever it was that was bothering you is now inconsequential.

The other benefit of blanking your mind is that you can do visualization. This is best done at night before going to sleep. Once your mind is blank, picture in your mind what it is that you want to accomplish. Do not force it. Just gently focus on the vision that you want to come to reality. Feel as if it is already accomplished. Do this every night. If done correctly, that vision will come to fruition before you know it.

To attain peace of mind, one must want it. The power is in all of us. Only you can make the decision to have the tranquility you desperately need. There is also one very important thing that you can do. Pray. Our God is a loving spiritual being that can help us in time of need. My faith in God is absolute and I feel blessed to have Him as my guide and teacher.

Stress and its ill effects

Stress is our normal physical and psychological reaction to an imagined or real stimuli. The ever increasing demands of modern life usually cause the stress in most people. If left unchecked, stress can turn into a chronic condition that results in significant negative consequences to our health. This decline can take the form of aches and pains, anxiety, chronic fatigue, depression, high blood pressure, gastrointestinal disorders like ulcers, heart disease, immune deficiencies, and other maladies.

Stress can kill. It almost did kill my sister. At the age of 36, my sister had a stroke. The neurologist was kind of preparing me for her demise because she had a bleed the size of a dollar in her frontal lobe and he said that this kind of hemorrhage was mostly fatal. However, I answered that I understood, but she was going to get well again. He drilled this into my mind two more times and I gave him the same answer.

My sister had emergency surgery to evacuate the bleeding. While in ICU, I brought her son to visit her. This freaked him out and he never went back. I had to ask my mother to come back so she could take care of her grandson.

Her rehabilitation was grueling. She had to relearn how to talk, how to eat properly so she did not choke on her food, how to walk, how to do the activities of daily living. She had physical, occupational, and speech therapy to guide her. She was wheelchair bound for a while. I was unemployed at the time. I felt it providential because I was able to stay with her at the hospital and care for her.

Living with a stroke survivor is not easy. It got to the point where I was ready to pull my hair out. Thank goodness for a colleague who had a similar experience and suggested we join a support group. I practically had to drag her because she did not want to go. The support group was our salvation.

Now my sister is permanently disabled. She is paralyzed on the left side of her body, but she is able to drive, go shopping, cook, and do laundry. The only thing she cannot do is go back to her former job of nursing. Her doctor would not allow it.

The stressors in her life were too much. She had a tumultuous relationship with her ex-husband. She was angry all the time, she let herself go, and gained a lot of weight. She just could not cope with being a single mom without any support as my mom went back home when my nephew turned six.

She had the stroke at work. Normally, that is the time she is driving for home. Thank goodness they had a meeting at work. She was rushed to Cedars-Sinai Medical Center and was attended to immediately. If she were on her way home, I would have lost two members of my family because she would have been in an accident due to the stroke. This is why I feel strongly about managing our stressors. If we take care of our stressors, that will prevent the catastrophic illnesses that can result if left unchecked.

The power of the mind

The *American Heritage College Dictionary* defines the mind as the human consciousness that originates in the brain and is manifested especially in thoughts, perception, emotion, will, memory, and inspiration.

Whenever we are awake, thoughts are never ending. They continually go on no matter what. Because thoughts are forces of energy, they impact and shape our lives and reality. Thoughts are constantly sent and received by the mind. If they are packed with emotions, they become magnetized and can attract similar thoughts. We have a choice to keep our thoughts or get rid of them. This constant chatter can be eliminated and replaced by positive thoughts we can use to our advantage as this will manifest in reality.

Below the conscious perception is the subconscious mind. This is where reality is created. This part of the mind does not know the difference between right and wrong. It picks up whatever thoughts and beliefs your conscious mind is thinking and it responds to the messages. It is the subconscious that is responsible in turning these thoughts into reality.

Because our mind is a force of energy, it can affect other people. If our mind is filled with anxiety, it will be felt by those around us. We can always do each other a favor if we would just keep good thoughts so the vibration in the place where we are in stays healthy.

Once the mind is cleared of the constant chatter, we can do visualization to help us achieve our dreams. I practiced visualization when I first arrived in America. All of us nurses that came as exchange visitors were required to take the State Boards. I wanted to make sure that I passed it on the first try because I didn't want to waste my time. Plus if I could do it on my first try, why not?

Every night before I went to bed, I would blank my mind and visualize that I was going to the mailbox. Once I opened it, I saw a white envelope; this meant that I had passed the State Board exam. I saw myself smiling broadly and happy. If the envelope was pink then it meant that you had to retake the exams.

Of course I did my part in making sure that I passed. Our class valedictorian told me that if I wanted to pass the RN exams, I had to read four hours a day. Also, we bet some money. Whoever failed had to pay up. Because I didn't want to lose, every day I would read my textbooks for three to four hours. I read two hours before going to work, squeezed in time for lunch and a shower, and then resumed reading for one to two more hours before going to sleep. I even took my book to work so that any chance I got, I read. Some people even said that if there's anyone who was guaranteed to pass, I was one of them. I did strict time management and worked on it and it paid off big time. One other thing that I did was I always made sure I prayed for guidance and enlightenment. The Lord was on my side then and up to this day. I feel so blessed.

This visualization technique I passed on to one of the LVNs in the Pediatric unit. When she failed the exam, she became a different person. She took her frustrations out on us, her coworkers. She used to be nice and helpful and fun to be around with. But when she did not pass the exams, she became a complainer. So I took her aside and told her that she need not be difficult; instead, if she wanted to pass the exams, she must read four hours a day. She needed to stop reading after two hours because the brain cannot absorb any more after that. I'm not sure now if I sent her a copy of the book that inspired me or if I suggested she get it and read it. Needless to say, after I had moved to California, she wrote me a letter stating that she had passed the exams. I was so happy for her.

The other wish that I had was to see my sister come to America. I put her through nursing school. When she finished her studies and wanted to come, I then proceeded to do my visualization. With her, I visualized her happily coming down from the airplane. I did this until she arrived. My wish came true because my sister wanted it, too. Visualization works only if the person you include in that image wants the same thing.

Get Rid of the Past

Know that we can only live in the present moment. The past is over and done with—let it go. Regretting what might have been does not help us in our growth as a person. If we live in the past or let it rule our life, it can affect us physically with life-threatening illnesses. It can lead to significant emotional and psychological problems as well.

Our mind is like a computer. Every life experience, good or bad, is kept within its confines and stays there. When life intrudes or a situation arises that reminds us of the past, what comes to the fore is what we already know. It will start the mind rolling again and revert to the experience of the past. If we dwell on it, the same scenario can influence our thought processes and distort our thinking. It will set you back instead of moving you forward. It's worse if it's something that you fear. Realize that whatever you fear comes true. That is how strong fear is.

This is especially true if someone has done you wrong or if you have committed something that in your mind is unconscionable. If you have not learned to forgive and forget, it will continue to fester and will affect you. It's worse if you hate a person. The person who is the focus of your hatred may not even know it, but you who harbors that hatred will suffer because it's deep inside of you and becomes like an obsession.

Same with failures. Whether it's work, business, marriage, personal accomplishments, if we want to move forward, we must leave it in the past and forget it. Because we failed does not mean that we cannot start over and improve ourselves. As long as our intentions are true and we are willing to correct the mistake, nothing can stop us from succeeding. Think of yourself as worthy of all the abundance that life has to offer.

The best thing that you can do is to be kind and forgive yourself. Once you do that, then you can forgive others who have offended you. Sometimes if the situation is grave and the negative experience occurred in your childhood years, if you have not come to terms with it on your own, seeking professional help will go a long way to help you get rid of the past.

In any endeavor, as long as we do not take advantage of someone else and follow the Golden Rule, success with peace of mind can be achieved. We are all capable of healing ourselves, breaking bad habits, and changing the way we think, feel, and act. When we do this, we can put an end to the emotional suffering and pain that affects not only us, but our loved ones as well.

Let bygones be bygones. Live and enjoy the life the good Lord has given you. Living in the past is not a healthy way to live. We must come to terms with it and move on. Our present and our future depend on it.

Don't worry

Worrying is an unhealthy and destructive habit. It's a result of fear of the future, which is another day, unborn and unreal. Because we live in a world of uncertainty, tension, and stress, we worry about circumstances that most of the time never come to pass.

It is an exercise in futility to worry about something you have no control of. Filling your thoughts with dread and negativity clouds your thinking and impairs your ability to concentrate and make decisions.

Getting rid of worry is an important skill to acquire. Only you can make a decision on whether you continue on worrying yourself sick or dealing with it. Replace fear with faith. Entrust your cares to the Lord. Let the power of prayer guide you and enlighten your mind.

Clear your mind regularly, especially before going to sleep. Once the mind is blank, fill it with thoughts of faith, hope, peace, and abundance. Visualize yourself as overcoming worry and fear. Because fear is the most powerful of all thoughts, it is important to replace it with faith/belief that everything will turn out for the best.

A calm mind can help tremendously in decision making. When worry comes knocking, make a decision to confront the worry head on. Get pen and paper and write down what exactly it is you are worried about, what you can do about it, decide on a course of action, and then carry out that decision. You will discover that worry vanishes once you have a thought-out plan of action to fix the problem.

Chronic worry can lead to insomnia and generalized anxiety disorders. Insomnia is a chronic condition wherein a person is unable to sleep or remain asleep throughout the night. The Consumer Union reported that pharmacists filled 43 million prescriptions for sleep medications in 2005, an increase of 32% from 2001. Profits to pharmaceutical companies was $2.7 billion.

Consumer Reports reported that 60% of their subscribers surveyed stated that they had trouble falling or staying asleep, or they woke up still tired at least three times per week. Job-related stressors were the common reason cited.

Since drugs have side effects, alternative methods to aid in having a good night's sleep include regular exercises, meditation, yoga, and deep breathing exercises.

Universal law states that we manifest into physical reality the thoughts and attitudes we hold in our conscious mind, no matter what they are. Attitudes shape our future. If our attitude towards ourselves and others are generous and kind, we will attract generous portions of success.

We have a choice in this ever-changing world we live in. I choose to have a positive mental attitude. I hope you will, too.

***

To Contact Frenee:

(562) 413-4921

amzn.to/118fCyy

Dr. James R. King

Dr. James R. King attended the University of Metaphysics Institute in Brooklyn New York from 1969 to 1976. He studied under Dr. David Potts, who was the Headmaster and Chief instructor, in addition to Siri Sat Nam Singh (Transcendental Kundalini Yoga Meditation), Dr. Rico Zoves (Studies in Healing Arts, Agnihotra Meditation, and in vibration, word, sound, and color therapy) and received his Doctorate in Metaphysical Studies. He was also awarded an Honorary Doctorate in Humane Letters and in Divinity from the Global Oved Dei University and Seminary in 2013 and currently serves as the Executive Director for Climate Change Studies at the newly reformed Olof Palme Peace Foundation International NGO-DPI at the United Nations in New York. Dr. King has a 40-year history in the study of the Shotokan System of Martial Arts. He is a songwriter and musician and is currently working on music production projects in New York. As a Lecturer and Author, he is currently a co-host on a Tuesday morning conference broadcast "The Billionaire Master Mind Forum," during which he does a weekly in-depth discussion on the book by Charles F. Haanel entitled *The Master Key System*. Dr. King is married with six brilliant children.

In Search of Humanity's Vision

Where Do We Go From Here?

By Dr. James R. King

Part ONE

I was the oldest of six children raised in Brooklyn, New York. I had other brothers and sisters on my dad's side in North Carolina that I didn't know about until I was twelve years old. We grew up in the BROWNSVILLE SECTION of Brooklyn in a sixteen-story building, one of eight in a housing project development called Samuel J. Tilden Houses.

Note: (picture upwards of 2,000 people within a 4 block area and limited resources—Tilden is one of nine projects within a one-mile radius)

One of the standout experiences I remember from my childhood was that my family had developed this drill to be followed any time we heard gang activity or gunfire outside of our first-floor windows. As soon as the shouting and gunfire started, we were rushed to turn off all of the lights and to go into a room in an area of the apartment that was less near the sound of fighting, told to lay or stoop down below the window sill and not to move until she told us to. My responsibility was to make sure that the rest of my sibs followed directions. I could feel the pain and hear the fear in the sounds of running, fighting, cursing, and screaming outside. From the back bedroom window, I could see across the project yard area to the streets surrounding the housing development and a number of things struck me as strange. First of all, my mom would be on the phone calling the police as soon as she heard any outbreak of gunfire or movement of gangs through the project area, which was more frequent during the summer months. The police seemed never to respond right away and during the "Gang Wars" they would surround the outlying areas of the projects (i.e., Livonia Avenue, Stone Avenue, Rockaway Avenue) and wait for the fighting to stop and all of the survivors to leave the area before they would slowly walk into the war zone to arrest the wounded and kick at the dead. And just as a sidebar, my dad was this kind of ghost type mover during all of these events. He worked usually until late evening and one of the family's main concerns was that he had to walk from the Rockaway Ave. Station and through the projects to get to our building, and we did not have cell phones to warn him. Now the reason I say "Ghost Like" is because it always seemed that the gangs would just stop fighting at the time his train got in the station at Livonia Ave., wait until just after he got into the house, and conclude shortly after so as not to disturb him. How did he do this? The surprise to me was to find out that there was something being done intently by him. I will cover that shortly.

I remember being afraid for my family, especially my brothers and sisters, and I remember not liking the feeling of fear, not even a little bit. This became a large part of what shaped my life's quest and purpose…..my hatred of FEAR.

I remember waking up the next day and looking at the news on television and after counting the number of bodies I saw being collected after the violence, there was no mention of any of it on the six o'clock TV news, the radio, or in the newspapers available to us at that time. I remember taking it personally and thinking that the reason these events were not important enough to cover was because we lived in a neighborhood that was predominantly Hispanic and Black and that in the eyes of the Media Controllers, we just were not important enough to get coverage—as if it were ever that simple. I mean think about it—the only black people we saw in mainstream media in the early years of our lives were Amos and Andy and Buckwheat from the *Little Rascals*. I remember when I got to school hearing of friends or parents who got caught outside and were killed during the conflict either coming from the store, the train station, from work, or just being in the yard at the time the shooting, stabbing, stomping, or clubbing started. The gang activity and deaths were just the tip of the iceberg.

We would attend services every Sunday with my dad as was part of my family ritual, all except my mom which was curious to me after I got older. Mom was a well-educated school teacher and program administrator with the NYC Board of Education. She was also what was at the time known as a Christian Scientist and her take on God and religion was different and interesting. To listen to the debates between Mom and Dad was always stimulating, though as a child I remember them arguing more than reasoning. They were both musicians, singers, played piano, and were excellent dancers, so to see them arguing about religion or money was always hurtful and in contrast to all of the beautiful and fun things we did together as a family.

I didn't figure out that we were poor until around high school, the reason being that my dad drilled into us that we had to learn a skill or some trade, work doing chores, and help out in some way in the house with the family and this was something that he and my mom did not argue about.

Being the oldest, you didn't get hand-me-downs. As a matter of fact, the world becomes REAL to you quicker. It seems to come at you from all sides. Your parents and their demands that you be an example to your sibs, from your sibs that you help and protect them from things and people who would abuse them physically and mentally, from the world with its expectations, from religions with all of its puzzles, and most of all from you in your attempts to fit in, figure it all out, and come out of it SANE.

Most of the arguments between my mom and dad were about money. My mom was a school teacher, but for years at the time of the birth of my younger brothers and sisters there was only one primary bread winner, my dad. I was looking for jobs to make my own money and found my first real job at thirteen years old, working part-time after school and on weekends. I met such a variety of people at my job, which was working in a men's and boy's chain store on Pitkin Avenue called ROBBINS as a stock clerk, setting up displays, tagging merchandise, loading and unloading trucks, sweeping, mopping, running errands and anything I was asked to do. One of the managers at the Brooklyn Store had asked me to fill in at their Midtown store in Manhattan. This grew to be every weekend. I met all types of people from all races, genders, religions, and attitudes from the worst to the best. I made my own money and learned early not to spend it, but to think in terms of using it. Now in learning, I did spend it on some of the most wasteful things you could imagine. Although working six days a week, going to school, taking martial arts classes, and playing piano kept the waste down to a minimum, wasting money and the lessons taught from the feelings of waste and regret were priceless. I learned to play piano, did my homework, joined a free Karate Club, and did everything I could to stay out of an overcrowded home situation and off the streets at the same time.

Death in Brownsville was something that you learned to get used to. The area where we grew up is still today one of the most densely impoverished areas in the country, and with this congestion came conflict. By the time I reached the age of nineteen, most of the children I knew growing up were dead or mentally challenged as the product of our surroundings. I remember getting to a point of not wanting to meet anyone new for fear that that I would like them and then they would die. Two of my brothers were murdered in the same development and so many friends, men and women, are dead or suffer from some kind of mental illness or physical disability. The awareness acquired and the lessons learned from the experience of ignorance, prejudice, poverty, doubt and despair, deceit, greed, lust and the fear that these realities created hurt me to the core. Pain in a way that threatened to drive me crazy and forced me to find the answer to the ever-raging question in my spirit "WHY are these things happening anywhere on GOD'S earth and WHAT WAS I GOING TO DO ABOUT IT?" This became a trigger phrase for me from childhood that developed from times when my brothers or sisters would come to me in tears and sometimes in blood after being attacked in the neighborhood. I never liked to fight and I would always try to find a peaceful way to resolve any conflict, until you said something that sounded like "Yea so what I threw a cherry bomb in the elevator while your sister was in there and so WHAT'RE YOU GONNA DO ABOUT IT?" Whenever I would hear such a statement, my response was always immediate. I have always been a great fighter when there was a good reason. Now I had reached a point in my life where I was asking myself *the question, WHY, for the whole of my life experience, WHY!*

Part TWO

I had access to a diversified library of not only the books we were required to read in order to graduate in school, but also from my mom and dad who were avid readers. One of the books that always puzzled me as a child was a book called *THINK AND GROW RICH* by Napoleon Hill, which was one of those books my mom had just lying around the house that I would pick up to read to keep from arguing over the one television shared by eight people. She had other books of interest to me as well, an English translation of the TORAH, her Bibles, and her various magazines from UNITY and The Christian Science Monitor. My dad's reading material was more in line of where I felt I would find the real answers to the things that were hurting me.

One afternoon I was going through my dad's books in the top of his bedroom closet, while he was at work, and I came across some pictures and this item reference in a book called *The Secret Doctrine* by H.P. Blavatsky which contained the following statement:

[The sixth item gives a core idea of theosophical {Divine Wisdom} philosophy, that "as above, so below". This is known as the "law of correspondences", its basic premise being that everything in the universe is worked and manifested from within outwards, or from the higher to the lower, and that thus the lower, the microcosm, is the copy of the higher, the macrocosm. Just as a human being experiences every action as preceded by an internal impulse of thought, emotion and will, so too the manifested universe is preceded by impulses from divine thought, feeling and will.]

Now let's bring this back to an everyday language of discussion and create the link needed to answer the question of "WHAT AM I GOING TO DO ABOUT IT?" Between the above statement and others I have read along the same lines, was I to believe that I could think in a certain way and change my life and the things in my surroundings and environment? Well what thoughts do I have to think? And let's for a shift change the question to "WHAT ARE WE GOING TO DO ABOUT IT" because I am quite sure about one thing—in my surroundings and environment there were others that I shared this reality with and in order for it to change I would need their help. We would have to think in concert to be successful. I was not the only one feeling pain from the hardship realities of this World.

Question: "What really killed my brothers" and what thoughts need to change to keep this same scenario from repeating itself in my life and the lives of others? Do we really write our own scripts and create our own realities?

Now it was just too simple and insulting for me to accept the reasoning that they, my brothers, were just BAD people and they deserved to die. They were in the wrong place at the wrong time. Nor to accept that drugs, guns, knives, baseball bats, being pushed off of the platform on 14th Street and Union Square in front of a train were the causes of their deaths or the death of anyone ever. Were the poverty level, gang violence, gambling, prostitution, racism, illiteracy, or any other outside circumstance truly the cause of the suffering and death that consumed the memories of my childhood? What was I missing? Was there something else?

The first brother's death was the younger one whom I felt that I should have been there to protect him. The second brother was one of the family members that I was introduced to after my 12th birthday who became my best friend, business partner, martial arts study partner, college roommate, and they both died within 18 months of each other.

I NEEDED ANSWERS ....NOW.

> *"Just as a human being experiences every action as preceded by an internal impulse of thought, emotion or will, so too the manifested universe is preceded by impulses from divine thought, feeling and will."*
>
> *The Secret Doctrine*

I had been hearing the statement that THOUGHTS ARE THINGS along with the idea that you could just THINK AND GROW RICH and at that point in my life, it was difficult to accept or believe. I did not know anyone who actually wanted the problems and tragedy they experienced. If our thoughts do create our reality, then I must be thinking the wrong thoughts. I began to read and then test my thoughts and compare thought to feeling in this way; I became a living laboratory. To some members of my family, it looked like I was really losing it. I would think a certain thought, act on it, and do a self-assessment. Measure the consequences of the action and monitor how it all made me feel as well as how it made other people feel. I observed people who were habitual liars feel better for a moment and not care how it made anyone else feel as long as they got what they wanted. I noticed that lying for me was uncomfortable and confusing me in just the action of trying to remember them all. I have witnessed the deaths of people who had lied and got caught. I had also seen people who were prideful, selfish, and greedy look successful and I watched others become jealous and envious of them. These people sometimes were drug dealers, pimps, hustlers and pastors. Upon observing the relatively short-term outcome of their situation, they would end up in jail or losing all of what they seemed to possess.

I began to identify the thoughts and the feeling of successful people and as I got older, I would use myself more as a test dummy to identify the thoughts and feeling that made me feel better.

One of the things we learned to do from early childhood was to PRAY, although even prayer had a question mark attached to it because I was praying to something or someone that I couldn't see and did not understand. It still made me feel better. In line with the prayer I identified other thoughts and actions that made me feel full and accomplished. Now again, I am on a mission to identify the difference in the thoughts that made me feel good versus the thoughts in the minds of the people who killed my brothers. For just a reminder, guns, knives, bats, weapons of any kind don't kill people….THOUGHTS KILL PEOPLE.

After 40 years of testing, observation of myself and others, and much prayer and meditation, I was able to determine through measured study as well as trial and error which kinds of thoughts and actions made me feel better and allowed me to accomplish more, and add more value to others, and which thoughts and actions made me sick of mind and body. I also monitored the effects on the people around me in various situations. I received confirmation for my findings from the likes of Jesus Christ, the Prophet Mohammad, my wife and children Sahuspete, Breyone, Kaiqwon, Irlyaan, Amina, Ausara Yah, Mahatma Gandhi, Rev. Dr. Martin Luther King,

The Change[9]

Wayne Dyer, Charles Haanel, Jim Rohn, Osoronko Nana Yabani, Sensei Minor of ISKF in New York, H.P. Blavatsky, Siri Sat Nam Sing, Napoleon Hill, and others.

(*Yes, your thoughts, feelings, words, and actions can make you sick or make you heal, can create success or failure.*) Now as a reminder, the type of research and development that I had to witness and endure was accomplished through my personal ignorance, extreme personal pain and hardship; in the full book version I will go into greater detail.

At this point, I am going to ask that you test my conclusions on yourself. Observe the actions, success, and failures of others throughout history and draw your own conclusions out of the results experienced in their lives. The following thoughts manifested results that were painful and counter-productive in measurable terms in my life and the lives of others as well. When the feelings associated with these thoughts become *obsessions,* they led to actions of murder and other criminal behavior, oppression, personal fear, disease, and the death of any circumstance or condition be it business, policy, family, community, or government where these feelings and attitudes were prevalent.

ENVY (the feeling of resentment and longing for someone else's possessions, qualities, or seeming good fortune)

DOUBT (self; a feeling of uncertainty or lack of conviction. To question the truth or fact of something)

SHAME (perceived loss of position, respect, or esteem. A feeling of humiliation, dishonor, or feeling outdone by a person or group of people)

PREJUDICE (a perceived opinion, not based on fact, reason, or actual experience)

SELFISHNESS (lacking consideration for others)

GREED (intense and selfish obsessive desire for something not needed, i.e., wealth, power, food, knowledge. There is no good greed)

ARROGANCE (having an exaggerated sense of one's own importance or abilities)

VANITY (excessive pride in or admiration of one's own appearance)

JEALOUSY (a wrongful desire for a person or thing that rightfully belongs to another)

DECEIT (the action of concealing or misrepresenting the truth)

LUST (a strong sensual desire, when obsessed becomes deadly)

PIOUSNESS (a hypocritical display of virtue, being outwardly religious without the application of moral truth and action in life's challenge)

Guilt, Laziness, Pity, Poverty, Grief, Pride (see Proverbs), Loneliness, Spite and Shyness.

These thoughts, when experienced over a prolonged period by any individual or group, become obsessions that lead to stress, resentment, anger, fear, anxiety, depression and despair, criminal activity, and in the end death and destruction of personal energy, health, wealth, hope, self-love, the love for family, friends, community, and creative expression.

The obsession of one or more of these thoughts and feelings were the weapons used to kill my brothers. As I said in the beginning, I needed to know what killed them and I needed to know why such senseless destruction is experienced anywhere.

All of these thoughts take value away from the person who is thinking them in the form of health, relationships, money, ideas, life span, and the overall quality of life.

The Change

To begin to answer the question "What are we going to do about all of the death and despair?" We start with identifying the thoughts and feelings associated with HEALTH, WEALTH, PEACE, PROSPERITY, UNITY, AND HOPE. We start at the beginning and in the beginning was the WORD......JOHN 1:1-5.

Ancient and modern science support the finding that everything vibrates and that the difference between the way that any object looks, feels, smells, or tastes like depends on the rate, mode, or pattern frequency of that object. When you take any thought and slow down its speed of vibration, it becomes WORD. Based on the intention of the word, it will take form, become real (*be made flesh*), in line with the understanding of the person receiving the word. Whether a person understands the meaning of a word does not diminish the power of the Words.

Being surgically selective of the words we think and speak is the true master key to change.

The following list includes Words of Action that when spoken or acted upon create images and inspire feelings of Hope and Healing in all areas of life relationships:

PATIENCE (the capacity to accept or tolerate delay, trouble, or suffering without becoming angry or upset: key word—faith)

PERSEVERANCE (steadfastness in doing something despite difficulty or delay: key word—grace)

INTEGRITY (the quality of being honest and having strong moral principles: the state of being whole and undivided: a condition of being unified, at one with Splendor, Truth, Severity, Boldness, Charm, Balance, Rhythm, Harmony, Strength, Courage)

Words that inspire feelings, actions, and visions of Victory, Healing, Success, and Abundance, these words are the definition of LOVE.

The surprising part to me was that my life changed when my words changed. All of the truths I was taught as a child and all of the pain endured began to form a pattern that made sense. The late Wayne Dyer had a saying that attracted me to him and which I think was one of his favorites, "WHEN YOU CHANGE THE WAY YOU LOOK AT THINGS, THE THINGS YOU LOOK AT CHANGE."

What also was made very clear through the hardship and pain was that the Divine God of the Universe, what I learned to refer to as INFINITE LIVING MIND, could radiate all of its power in one word—"Love"—and in Love we HEAL.

I finally figured out how my dad was able to walk through the projects like a Ghost, untouched and with no fear.

***

To Contact James:

E-Mail: www.thequilizer@gmail.com

Tel- 718 314 3348

Kathryn Wilking

Kathryn Wilking is an Author, Stager and Feng Shui Consultant, with a 25-year background in the decorating and home improvement industry. As a specialist in paints and coatings, she moved into consulting and project management roles, after completing college business studies.

Kathryn discovered feng shui in 1998, and soon realized it could fulfill her need to work on a deeper, personal level with her clients. Through feng shui, she found answers to help her personally, and insight to fill her client's needs. Kathryn shows clients how fresh energy can create new opportunities, a positive outlook, better relationships, and good health.

In the following chapter, Kathryn starts by sharing her early experience working intimately with people as a dance instructor. This direct contact with different personalities gave her insight on how various types of people learn and interact. Moving into consulting services provided the opportunity to grow and expand this knowledge.

An active Professional Member of the International Feng Shui Guild, Kathryn is available for private consultations, talks, and workshops. Kathryn has a monthly newsletter and a blog that focuses on office and business-related topics.

The Fantastic Five: Find the Answers, Get the Advantage

By Kathryn Wilking

I was barely out of high school in the mid-1970s when I ran away to join the circus!

I was never encouraged to go to university or told that I would ever be a "somebody." The choices laid out for me were a nurse, secretary, or a school teacher; until I got married, of course. But I wanted to do something more: practical, yet unique, and I needed more direction. I didn't fit into the mold that pre-decided my fate in life, and I struggled with finding my true path.

I read the book *Think and Grow Rich* by Napoleon Hill, but was not convinced I could ever "think and grow rich." Instead, I adapted the phrase "Fake it until you make it." I was young, and did not have the advantage of life experience, but I quickly learned a lot about success and failure.

I didn't actual join a circus; I answered an ad in the newspaper for disco dance teachers (training provided). The ad specified: must be able to work evenings and weekends, and enjoy working in a party-type atmosphere. I was hired to teach at Fred Astaire Dance Studios on the spot. And yes, it was a bit of a circus!

I tell this part of my story because the five years I spent teaching dance and in competitions was all about working intimately with the general public. It was a tremendous experience and gave me insight on how to interact with all types of personalities. At that time, our sales strategy was based on recognizing the difference between A-type people and B-type people, as extraverts and introverts needed to be treated in a different way. But the format was way too rigid—people are much more complex than that.

Not only did I have to remain upbeat and positive all the time, I had to teach. And I had to continue to set goals with my clients in order to "sell up." Selling a package was either progressive, to proceed to the next level of dance instruction, and/or prepare for dynamic competitions.

I was fortunate to see many students develop confidence, on more than just the dance floor. They also learned to stand up for themselves and walk tall while they moved forward into life's challenges. It was very rewarding.

After five years of the dance circus, I left the studio life. There were tough times ahead: the recession hit, my mortgage came up for renewal at 21.5%, my husband (and dance partner) and I were fighting regularly, and I found out I was going to have a baby!

I lost my house, my husband, and the business in 1981. Looking back, it was okay to walk away. It was time to regroup.

I was hired as an Assistant Manager in a retail paint and wallpaper company. Why? Because they were hiring and I liked decorating. Within six months, the company sent me to manage a store in small-town Welland, Ontario. At 23 years old, I was in over my head. The store had previously "gone bad" and the company pulled the franchise; I was sent into a hornet's nest. The employees were not happy, but were told they could keep their jobs. My designated "assistant" was off on a medical leave as she just had a hysterectomy. Geez....I got down to work.

Pushing all the baggage and poor reputation aside, I managed to turn around this rundown store, and make a profit. The head office decided not to close the store.

I can't claim all was smooth over the next five years; I did have personal issues. Long-time loyalties run deep and my young age did not help. I was still managing "by myself" rather than tapping into the others' experiences. I had much to learn about managing people and that there are human beings involved. There is a balance between perfectionism and practicality, and there is a place for compassion.

Over the next ten years, I bounced from retail gig to college, to consulting, and back; as well as teaching dance as a hobby. It was employment, unemployment, self-employment and repeat… there were tough times… recession, divorce, feast or famine.

One day I read an article in the newspaper that talked about "The Average 'Joe Canadian' is actually a Jane!" I was stunned! The description of the "average Canadian" was ME! I was female, age 32, divorced, with a single child. The income bracket matched, even my height and weight matched… it was weird.

I wondered, "Geez, I'm only average?" If I was destined for greatness, I had to get out of town and find another path.

So, with this reflection, I figured that I could continue on my rollercoaster ride of feast and famine, or pick a quieter road; one that was a little gentler on me, and where I would be happy. I didn't want to beat myself up about NOT going anywhere anymore.

It was 1998 when I re-married to a wonderful engineer, who also came with a little boy. We combined our households, and I found it difficult to sort out and arrange our accumulation of items. This was the first time I reached out to a feng shui consultant. Feng shui helped to organize my life, sort out priorities, and find the balance in my day-to-day world. Feng shui—the art of placement, manipulation, and energy—came into my life!

So I added a hat to my disguise. Along with being an entrepreneur, manager, consultant, paint specialist and dance teacher….I was studying feng shui. I was still looking for that edge, still reaching for that shiny star that would explain what I was supposed to do.

It wasn't until we moved to Vancouver, BC in 2006 that I knew I needed to be properly certified in order to live a total feng shui lifestyle. Now, as a professional member of the International Feng Shui Guild (IFSG), I can consult and share with others around the world in this positive energy movement.

There are many misconceptions about feng shui; it is more than flower arrangements and gold coins. It is really very logical. This ancient art is about manipulating energy and energy patterns. Feng shui has a Buddhist influence reflecting ethics, morals, and practicality; the basis of living harmoniously in our surroundings. There are many fascinating insights to feng shui that can help repair relationships, and build abundance in your life. Through one concept, the Five Elements Theory, I discovered a real truth, and figured out what was wrong with my world and my life. I call them the Fantastic Five!

The Five Elements Theory is related to natural elements: wood, fire, earth, metal, and water; each one with its own tangible qualities of shape, color, number, body part, direction, season, and more. My aha moment came when I realized that these elements can also relate directly to personalities! These five elements can be used as a tool to understand yourself and your relationships.

When you learn to recognize the character traits relating to these natural elements, they will reveal all sorts of patterns. You will probably recognize a dominant-element within yourself right away, or perhaps you identify with more than one. The ideal would be to develop skills in all of these elements in order to maintain a balanced life. With experience, you will be able to identify these elements within others, and with this wisdom, you can choose how to handle each of life's situations as they arise.

Wood-people are extraverts: lively, energetic, physical, impulsive, bold, and engaged with society. They make great salespeople, entrepreneurs, and have great ideas for growth and change. They are instinctive motivators, movers, and shakers.

How to remember? Think of a tree growing and changing, adapting to the seasons: Flexible at times, intense periods of growth, and supporting wildlife.

Fire-people are also extraverts: driven, passionate, outspoken and dramatic. They make great spokespersons, actors, or politicians, gathering fuel for their cause. They love the spotlight.

How to remember? Think of an actual fire; lively people who command attention. They can sometimes be disruptive, and time-consuming to work with.

Earth-people are arbitrators: kind, nurturing, compassionate, loyal, and patient. They are calm in a stormy situation. You can find them working as a teacher, life coach, customer service reps, and in human resources. They love to volunteer or serve on a social committee.

How to remember? Think of an earth-mama; they know when something isn't right and try to fix it. They keep meticulous lists in order to include everyone in their plans/gatherings, offering refreshments at every occasion.

Metal-people are introverts: reserved, loyal, trustworthy, and have an eye for details. They thrive in the health care industry, finance, banking, the legal field, engineering, and computers. They are the backbone of society.

How to remember? Think of a metal object: heavy and hard to move. They are great at following policy and procedures; inflexible and only malleable if motivated under severe pressure.

<u>Water-people are also introverts</u>: They are the quieter ones. Just like deep water: reflective, hard to move, pontifical, full of great wisdom, and critical of change. They make great authoritative figures: judges, bank managers, corporate board of directors, presidents, etc. Water-people usually have the power to delegate tasks to others.

How to remember? Think of deep, calm water containing the experience of a lifetime… slower moving, wise, and thoughtful about the impact of actions on the future.

While we all have our strengths and weaknesses, the idea is to recognize and develop our weak areas and curb some of our dominant traits. To maintain a balance in all these elements will allow you to connect with all types of people.

The Five Elements are arranged in a specific order, with the ability to support or destroy one another. Why they are so fantastic is because the "support cycle" of these elements can help to insure a proper balance in the world:

Wood feeds the fire.

Fire consumes and forms ash/earth.

Earth compresses to create metals.

Metal can be melted and forged to carry water.

Water nurtures wood to continue life.

More intense study reveals another cycle: the destructive cycle. When the elements don't line up, competition, friction, and disruption can occur. We see this easily in nature, but we don't automatically recognize this in people. When we do, it's very revealing:

Wood (people) can break through/overwhelm earth (people).

Earth (people) can dam/bury water (people).

Water (people) can drown/destroy fire (people).

Fire (people) can melt/disfigure metal (people).

Metal (people) can damage/chop wood (people).

This seems pretty intense. And, it is! When you are in a situation that is uncomfortable, chances are, someone is pushing your dominant-element into action or reaction.

The groundbreaking clues I needed to better understand myself came when I looked back into my past and dissected problematic issues, with the five elements perspective. I looked at my own dominant and non-dominant elements. I took the time to reflect on every employer I had in the past. I looked at the people I could get along with, and people I had issues with. I replayed conversations that went right, and went wrong… and then I looked at my family.

I finally got it! The dynamics that stared at me were clear—I am a wood-dominant-person. Wood-people can get told shut up and sit down, don't make waves, and that their ideas are stupid. It is no wonder that I've felt some people ganging up on me. As a wood-person, I know now, I have a problem with some metal-people.

I learned to recognize my weaker elements along with my strong wood-element. And, I learned how to recognize the elements of those around me; how to handle these issues in order to work harmoniously.

I put together a Personal Element Profile (PEP Quiz) to help other people find these answers within themselves. I started talking about personality dynamics and office yin and yang. I was convinced this could make a breakthrough in building teams, hiring the right people, partnering with the right people, and SELLING to the right people!

Through feng shui, I've booked talks and workshops on how to build teams and manage winning projects: it is all about interpersonal dynamics that can be related back to the five basic elements of nature. This amazing insight into personalities can reveal strengths and weaknesses in yourself, and those you work with; to the benefit of both your office and home life.

Feng shui has brought out the gentler side in me. I'm no longer as upset if things go wrong; I can explain them away with a thought, "Well, they are a metal-person." And, I know they can hurt me; but only if I allow it.

My management style has changed over the years from a task-oriented type of boss to one that realizes the human side has to show up from time to time. I've had only a few disgruntled workers over my career and one thing I had to develop is a deep respect for each one of them. People tend to bring their personal issues to work and that will always affect job performance. Managers must be prepared to wear many hats, in order to solve problems and issues of the day.

A manager may have the same goals as the team, but be aware that the team will change as they grow. Some people work better when they have clear objectives and are left alone, and others need more confidence in order to make decisions. A manager needs to recognize these skills to be accountable for the whole team and learn how to manage change as things move forward.

So, why do we resist change?

The main reason is fear; fear of the unknown. If everything is comfortable and everyone knows what to expect, why upset the balance? Because things are going to change regardless and we tend to worry about the outcome. Change can be stressful. A move can represent an insane amount of stress, and yet, it can lead to more avenues to explore, things to learn, and opportunities to develop.

The Change[9]

Energy changes from season to season, weekly, daily, and moment by moment. We are all in this world of change, as nothing stays the same. If we can grow and be flexible with our changes and the changes going on around us, we will have achieved something that not everyone can do.

I've come a long way from teaching dance lessons at the disco. The Fantastic Five Elements give me a tangible: something to see and something to work with that makes practical sense. The elements have bonded, acted, and reacted with each other for centuries, and we can learn a lot about human nature through these natural relationships. Yes, I may be demographically "normal," yet I have a message to deliver to the world. The advantage is all about balancing the energy and how we need to get along with others. And, with this knowledge, the world should be a better place to live.

I've incorporated feng shui into my lifestyle and my business since 1998. As a Feng Shui Consultant, I can help people not only organize their physical space to support their goals, but I can advise how to set up space that will support different personalities. Each individual will have a different path to success in hiring teams, choosing a partner, and building their support system.

My thoughts, my words, and my actions are reflected in a blog, a newsletter, and published books: in 2013, *Practical Feng Shui for the Office; Finding Your Individual Balance in the Work Place*. And in 2015, *Taking Command of Your Business: 27 Insights to Help You Thrive*.

For more information as to how the Fantastic Five Elements can help you with your business and your life, contact me. I'd be delighted to help you on the journey to find balance and harmony in your world.

***

To contact Kathryn:

Kathryn Wilking Designs

778-558-2693

www.kathrynwilking.com

kathryn@kathrynwilking.com

www.practicalfengshuifortheoffice.com

Kristin Marie Ecklund

Kristin Marie Ecklund is a catalyst for clarity and transformation. She brilliantly helps dissolve confusion, insecurity, and negativity and enables reconnection with the Source of certainty, peace, and joy.

Kristin's unique gift is to facilitate potent insights into why things aren't working so her clients can make choices and get their lives back on track. With her laser-focus guidance, limitations that once seemed insurmountable easily disappear.

Kristin is able to unearth mental programs with great ease and comfort. Clients experience unconscious baggage dropping away with calmness replacing discomfort and pain.

Kristin opens her clients' lives to tremendous possibilities, more quickly and easily than many have imagined possible. Working with Kristin facilitates feelings of peace, centeredness, and certainty about next steps. Clients gain awareness about the ego-based monkey mind lies that limit true genius.

Kristin is a natural-born intuitive who developed her abilities and gained a vast knowledge of spiritual healing and holistic coaching with over 15 years of professional training as well as experience with her own incredible life transformation. She also holds a Masters in Management from Northwestern's Kellogg Graduate School of Management and an undergraduate degree in Finance from the University of Wisconsin – Madison.

Three Keys to Unlock Your Inner Genius

By Kristin Ecklund

Here is one thing I absolutely know to be true—no matter who you are, no matter what your upbringing, and no matter how you may currently feel about yourself—you are a genius.

Every single person on this planet is a genius when they show up as who they really are, whether it be loudly, softly, blazingly larger than life, or with a contained gentle stillness.

Let me be clear. Genius is not intellect. It's not having a ton of information. It's not being extraordinarily creative. What I mean by genius is being tapped into the Truth of who you really are at your very core. It's looking in the mirror with love, feeling internal respect, and being grounded and centered no matter what comes your way. It's about living with total integrity and feeling completely authentic and real.

That's living your genius potential. From there, all things are truly possible.

A genius is someone who is unapologetically him or herself 100% of the time. In that realness, the brilliance and beauty rises to the surface along with a willingness to be completely vulnerable. Life itself takes on a new flavor, and it tastes orgasmically good.

Through many years of working on myself and with others, I have reached of place where I live in my zone of genius, and the contrast is remarkable. This is why I'm so passionate about sharing how I made such an amazing change.

For many years, I lived as a limited version of myself, deeply trapped in cycles of limitation where happiness seemed illusive. But

I learned to break through the walls that prevented joy. I moved from a home I didn't feel safe in, a relationship that had fallen flat and at times was outright abusive to a place that my heart calls home and a relationship that is deeply loving and mutually respectful. Where life used to be a constant struggle, it now feels fluid. I love my life, and miracles abound.

One thing stands in front of people who haven't yet discovered their genius. It's stories. Stories about who we think we are and the energetic belief systems that we've built up around these stories. The stories become like walls, and the beliefs are the mortar that fortify them. These walls can become very, very thick and very, very tall.

These walls aren't visible, but they're effective in blocking a deeper understanding of ourselves and our connection with others. Sometimes we feel them intensely. We recognize when someone's got their guard up. But the walls that create the most impact are the ones that aren't obvious. These are the ones that take some work to dismantle, but when we do, the freedom is just as intense.

People who do the work and are willing to open themselves up to dismantle false beliefs will discover their inner genius. This is a fact.

In the years that I have worked with clients, I have found that that there are three simple steps that when taken allow one's genius to shine. These steps can be cataclysmic and defy all of what our "good senses" say is possible, or they can seem like the most infinitesimally small movement in some unknown direction.

Neither type of change is better, as both lead to positive outcomes. The thing that matters most and provides the greatest results is diligence—a willing to take these steps into the unknown. You see, it can be like learning a new language that very few people speak or walking into a dance class when you aren't sure if you've got one left foot or two.

The Change[9]

The prerequisite here is a desire to want something better for yourself and a willingness to create change, even if the current step feels smaller than a baby's step.

What I know to be true is that every single thing we do with an intention to surrender the heavy lie of mediocrity will open the gateway of true potential, and we cannot know for sure which step will cause it to swing wide open. Intention is critical.

Intend to know the truth of who you really are, and you will, most likely sooner than you can imagine possible.

Step#1: "I Am Willing" Mantra

This step requires one simple thing: a declaration to the Universe that you are willing for something better.

We do this by saying aloud these three words, "I Am Willing."

This may be the simplest thing you'll ever do and the most profound step you can take. The truth is, if you've set an intention to discover who you really are, you are already willing. In fact, the choice to read this is a sign of willingness. But making this declaration, whether it be out loud or silently inward, you set into motion new possibilities.

But here's the thing, don't just say the words—feel them.

To create really amazing synchronicities, where things start to happen and opportunities open up like magic, say them to yourself, out loud in front of a mirror. Say, "I Am Willing" for as long as it takes until the words feel good and your heart opens wide. By then, you won't want to stop.

Why?

Because saying these words with feeling, truly believing them, begins to melt the walls.

And, no, it doesn't require being willing for something specific. It's about recalibrating your frequency to be willing. That's all.

Let me share with you an example of what can happen when you step into truly being willing.

I worked with a beautiful woman recently who turned her life around with this step alone. Paige is a talented, highly creative designer, but when we started our work together, she was so blocked that she had lost her ability to create. No matter what she tried, she felt no inspiration, and that terrified her. On top of that she felt tired, unattractive, bored, and addicted to social drinking and cigarettes. Paige suffered from self-imposed misery arising from a hidden core belief of being worthy of nothing better. She'd do things to ease her pain, but it seemed that every step forward was followed by at least one backwards, and she was ready to give up.

I told Paige about the possibility of creating change, but that she had to be willing to go for it and not let setbacks deter her. It sounded almost impossible, but when I offered her the "I Am Willing" mantra exercise, she agreed to give it a try.

That's when things got interesting.

Within a few days, her heavy load felt like it was mysteriously lifting. Miraculously, she no longer wanted to get drunk with her friends and within days she decided to quit smoking. Paige began to regain her confidence, and the shakiness that had been a constant in her voice barely registered. Her boss, who had been highly critical, began to openly compliment Paige for her contribution. Friends reappeared in her life, some showing up with gifts and providing things she had been secretly wanting. The greatest thing I noticed was that the light inside her turned back on.

Why would a simple mantra, "I Am Willing," make such an impact?

Because at the core it engages what is true. "I Am" is a statement of truth. I Am. You Are. It engages the truth hidden beneath the persona and belief systems about who you think you are. It engages a deeply connected Source far beyond what the thinking mind can understand. It taps into your soul essence—the Source of your highest wisdom that is intimately aware of how creation truly functions.

Willingness is about invoking Divine Will, which is the essence that drives everything important and meaningful in life. Being willing is like standing on the highest mountaintop, reaching your arms up, opening wide, and declaring that the Source of All is welcome into your heart and that you're willing to listen and follow its guidance. Once it enters, there is little room for the little ego self to take control. Ego, the source of mediocrity and lies, doesn't disappear, but it does get quiet enough for the true voice to be heard. The ego feeds on lies, but your divine will shines the light on ego, causing it to recede.

Say slowly and with feeling, "I Am Willing." Notice the stillness that awakens.

If the ego monkey mind attempts to take over, say it again.

"I Am Willing."

Sit back and savor the stillness.

If the stillness doesn't come right away, wait. Let this be a slowly repeated mantra until the quietness settles in, and then say it even slower, with less frequency. Repetition can be necessary, and for those who take this on, the rewards are great. You don't have to be still for it to work. Be in movement if that feels good. It works the same.

Contained in that stillness is great knowledge, Divine Wisdom. It expands the mind beyond what the intellect can imagine and connects you with Infinite Knowing.

Step #2: Surrender What's Not Working

Once you decide to be willing, the next step is to make choices that create joy. This means letting go of what's not working. Letting go is a movement forward. It creates an energy that swings the door open so you can see what's behind it.

How do you know what to let go?

First, acknowledge what is.

That's where Paige began. After she stepped into willingness, she discovered what didn't feel good. This is facing reality. Doing this takes courage, but here's the thing. The moment Paige took note of what wasn't working, she entered into choice about it. Until then, she was living in a "no choice reality."

Being in a no choice reality is like living robotically.

Take note of what's happening in your life. Do you like where you live? How do you feel about your key relationship? Does your job fill you with a sense of passion and purpose? Are you living in abundance or lack?

Pick one area of your life, and don't let this be overwhelming. Simply note the outcomes, experiences, and things that are less than desirable, and don't worry. We won't stop there. This isn't going to be a complaint fest. It's about getting real in the present to create change in what comes next.

Would you be willing to write these down? It will help with what comes next.

Some of these things can be pretty emotional. Give yourself some deep belly breaths, notice what you feel, and decide to surrender what doesn't feel good. Imagine tossing all those yucky energies into a fire pit, and surrender them now. Start to imagine life without them.

If your mind gets stirred up with an uncomfortable thought, say this immediately: "STOP, CANCEL, DELETE." When said with conviction, this little phrase has the power to stop energetic mind impulses in their tracks and will erase them entirely and reprogram your mind.

When you look at your list of Don't Wants, decide they're just words, and rather than allowing them to feel bad, let them be catalysts for showing you what you DO desire instead. This is important. Take what you don't like and turn it around.

For example, if you've written "my boss doesn't treat me with respect," ask yourself "What would I like to experience instead?" Go for the opposite and make it as big and wonderful as you can imagine without limits. Write what you do want on a separate page from the "don't want" items.

Be as specific, detailed, and elaborate as you can with what you desire. Doing this literally begins to rewire your brain to allow for things that feel good.

Many people focus on what they don't like and complain about it. Doing this can only bring more of the same, because it keeps the frequencies alive that create these experiences. People who unlock their genius are willing to give up one of the biggest, most prevalent addictions in the world: the addiction to complaining and being a victim of circumstances. They are willing to turn things around by declaring what they desire, no matter how crazy it may sound in the moment, even to themselves.

Paige started to take a good deep look at her life. She went through the exercise listing all of the things that weren't working or didn't feel good. One by one, she turned them around, allowing herself to open to positive outcomes, some of which she couldn't even imagine possible at the time. For example, where she noticed that a friendship felt superficial, she wrote, "I have friends who are there for me and love me unconditionally." Once all the negative items were turned around, she burned that old list.

This exercise, "What do I want?" is about opening up new possibilities. Suspend disbelief and imagine how you'd like things in your life to be. Doing this shifts the energy from creating more of what you don't want to allowing things you do. It puts you in choice with the Universe, and you become its co-creator. Imagine how amazing it is to create with the Universe as your partner and guide!

Are you willing to give it a go?

It's your choice.

We can complain about the negative things in our lives, or we can focus on what we would rather have. It's our choice, and choice creates our reality. Trust me. I used to be one of the biggest complainers on this planet. I know how addictive that can be, and I also know how much easier life is when I turn it around.

Step #3: Follow the Lightness

Choice creates awareness, and awareness is the guide that leads you on your path each step of the way. Making a choice creates a receptivity and a partnership between you and the universe. Awareness is the lightbulb inside your heart that gives you the ability to know what feels good and what doesn't. It's about being tuned in to keep that which you like and let go of that which you don't.

At this point, you're in the dance. You're willing, you've made a choice by declaring what you desire, and then you watch for what happens next. This step is about being aware of how things feel and following the path of lightness.

Why?

Because people who are living their genius follow what feels good. They make choices that create an expansive feeling, because that's how life itself expands. It's how they continue to open up more and more possibilities for positive outcomes and how they unlock even more genius in everyday living.

Feeling good is an indication of being on your path and living in alignment with your highest potential. It's a sign that you are unlocking your inner genius.

This is a fact. Things that feel good, expansive, or light are indications of truth. Things that resonate heavy, constrictive, or unpleasant are indicators of lies. When we tap into this way of knowing, our genius leads the way. Know that what's true for you isn't universal, but it is for you, and that's what matters.

Would you like to test this out?

Ask yourself, "Am I filled with possibility?" Simply asking this question can feel beautifully light. Good questions hold keys to new ways of being. Tune in. What feels more expansive, "yes" or "no?"

When you make a decision, you get spiritual information. Sometimes it comes as a flash of knowing, and sometimes it's a download that you get over time. Let's say you've never tasted pistachio ice cream. You can stand in front of the freezer wondering what it might be like, or you can open the carton and give it a taste.

This is what life is like. When you make a choice, you set energy in motion. Declaring what you desire works like that, too. It opens possibilities. Things show up. Your job is to keep tuning in and follow the lightness. Ask questions and trust that the direction that feels best will create expansion and begin to unlock your inner genius. This is how to create miracles in your life.

When you feel stuck or you're not sure what to do, ask open-ended questions for which there are no predetermined answers.

Let's say you are feeling bad about something that's happened, and you can't stop feeling bad about it. You can ask, "What is this?" "Can I change it?" "How can I change it?" or "What else is possible here?" Pause between each question and allow the stillness to occupy the space.

Simply asking questions can change how you feel. This is how it worked for Paige. When things started to feel stuck she'd ask, "Am I willing for something better?" Her "yes" allowed her to rise on top of the wave that previously would have crashed down upon her.

When you tune into what feels the most expansive, choose it and take action quickly, because these are pivotal moments when you're on to something big. It's a bizarre phenomenon, but excitement, one of the most expansive feelings there is, can also seem scary. These emotions ride on the same neural paths.

But here's the thing. When you dare to lean into the excitement and choose what you know quickly, things work out in magical ways. It's another beautiful phenomenon...called a miracle.

People with lives where everything turns to gold and who make an extraordinary impact on the world or who are simply amazingly happy are the ones who have unlocked their genius. They're not special or unique. They have simply stepped into an ability that we all have, which is to be brilliant without apology. The steps to get there aren't hard. It begins with a genuine willingness to surrender and then follow what feels light.

So...are you ready to begin?

***

To Contact Kristin:

312-715-7811

www.kristinecklund.com

www.kristinmariehealing.com

https://www.facebook.com/kristin.marie.ecklund

Lyn Smith

Lyn Smith – (The Queen of HEARTS) - International Relationship Coach.

Lyn spent most of her life growing up and living in England and currently lives in Spain. As a teenager, she was subjected to several traumatic experiences that went on to impact her ability to trust, love, and enjoy relationships with men, for many years.

She has a proven track record as an International Relationship Coach & Inspirational Speaker over the past 30 years, based upon her own vast personal research, experiential learning, and trainings with the world's leading industry experts.

Understanding the polarization of masculine & feminine energy resulted in her creating massive attraction and a passionate intimate relationship—feeling alive, fulfilled, and at peace; inspiring her to design & present her own course programs to share these breakthrough relationship techniques with women across the globe.

Lyn's extensive experience includes coaching women from diverse backgrounds—regardless of their sexual orientation—both nationally and internationally; creating lasting love, passion, intimacy, fulfilment, and peace in their personal relationship.

Lyn makes a difference by helping you make a difference; she has a vision of contributing back on a global scale.

To enjoy a full, intimate relationship at its highest level, read her story…….

Survive, Heal, & Thrive 'Rape & Sexual Abuse'

By Lyn Smith

I want to inspire you to create/ attract your Ultimate Intimate Soul Mate Relationship. My expertise of Survive, Heal & Thrive 'Rape & Sexual Abuse' came about because it's very relevant to my own story.

My personal history is a very harrowing one. I didn't have a close relationship with my parents; as kids, we were seen and not heard. They were strict disciplinarians & didn't spare the rod when it came to corporal punishment. They always fought a lot and I remember one time when I was about 13 years old, my dad sent me to run after my mother to tell her to come back because she'd stormed out after yet another major argument.

When I caught up with her, she said through her own pain and anger, "Go away, I wish you had never been born!" words which shook me to the core and I've never forgotten since; negatively impacting my future image of myself as being unworthy of being loved because I believed that if my own mother didn't love me, how could anyone else and how could I love myself?

Words of wisdom—Take responsibility for loving yourself first

Then through my teens, I experienced several sexually traumatic events that no girl or woman should ever have to go through; I was raped at the age of 15 by a man who was someone I trusted at my local swimming club. I was a virgin and naïve enough to think that he offered me a lift home out of kindness!

That lift cost me the rest of my childhood, a potential competitive swimming career, my education, some good friendships as well as my femininity & dignity. It left me feeling violated, ashamed, and dirty! So I didn't tell a soul (until I was 42!).

Words of wisdom—You have a choice and a voice

I tried to pretend it never happened and for a while it worked. Then at 18, just when I was starting to trust men again, I was drugged and raped by a friend of my then boyfriend. I remember vividly how helpless & vulnerable I felt, and then to compound it all shortly afterwards my mum left my dad. In her absence, my dad in his pain & despair molested & tried to take advantage of me—fortunately I was able to escape from his clutches before yet another potentially serious sexual assault took place!

Words of wisdom—Determination to survive adversity is your greatest strength

This event sent me over the edge and I remember as a result distinctly planning my own suicide. It would have been very easy for me to do; at the time I was working as a Veterinary Nurse and lived in accommodation above the surgery. I had access to the poisons cupboard and recall going as far as reaching for a drug used to immobilize horses, which I knew would be fatal to me.

However, for some reason, 'something within me' stopped that happening; I believe it was the thought of leaving behind my younger brother, who was distraught at my parents' separation and already trying to cope at age 16 with an absent mother and my dad's excessive aggressive mood swings.

Words of wisdom—Trust and listen to your inner self

At age 19, I joined the Police Force; upon reflection I feel this was motivated by some hidden thought that if I couldn't get justice for myself, then maybe I could contribute in getting justice for others.

Sadly it only proved to be the reverse and I witnessed many guilty offenders getting off with little or no punishment.

I left after 5 years' service and thereafter began my passion in various careers in education, coaching, and training.

For all that, I know I'm not alone; many of you reading this will—and can—relate.

In the 1970s, children in the UK didn't have resources like 'Childline' to turn to for help. So I suffered in silence for 27 years before plucking up the courage to start my healing & personal development journey, and in 2002 I rang 'Rape Crisis.'

Guess what? After an initial assessment consultation during which I was told that "I looked like a typical rape victim," my consultant then pointed out after lengthy questioning that I was overweight (I've yo-yo'd up and down the scales all my adult life) wore black shapeless clothes, didn't wear makeup or nail varnish (and still don't), didn't wear perfume or any jewelry (and have only done so minimally in recent years).

She then continued, "This is because you're subconsciously trying to protect yourself and make yourself unattractive to men" and although it sounded harsh, on reflection I knew she was right! Then came the really devastating body blow—she ended the consultation by saying, "Sorry there is a waiting list; it'll be 12-18 months before a counsellor will become available!" Not what I wanted to hear after feeling I was finally ready to talk!

Words of wisdom—You can heal your life (Louise Hay)

Hopefully things have now positively progressed beyond my experience in the UK and worldwide in general.

Needless to say, all these experiences had a very negative impact on my intimate relationships. I remember having a promiscuous phase prior to meeting my ex-husband.

I desperately wanted love and to feel lovable. I made the mistake—as do many girls—of using sex to get this need met; so I went from not caring about my welfare and feeling totally needy & out of control (which only resulted in more hurt and distrust of men) to unconsciously looking for a man (my ex-husband) who would offer me protection, safety, love, stability, and who would also let me take total control of the relationship.

I got my wish, for the 23 years that I was with my ex-husband I was very controlling; I acted superior to him, forced my opinion over his, told him how to do things that he was perfectly capable of doing himself, and altered the things he did so they were done my way. I also wore an invisible suit of armor and was for the most part a cold frigid bitch!

Words of wisdom—Confusion comes before a breakthrough (Anthony Robbins)

All this was driven by my unconscious need to look after and protect myself on the back of not trusting men. What I ended up with was a man who I'd managed to emasculate on a regular basis. After years of inadvertently 'changing' him to become a male version of myself, I wondered why I didn't find him as attractive anymore; it's because I was the dominant one wearing the trousers (or pants).

I subsequently divorced this perfectly good man, not because I wasn't happy, but because I felt there was something missing. (I felt he had lost his balls, but it was me that had all but castrated him!) I felt unfulfilled. There was no passion and although there was love & intimacy in the main, we had a 'friendship' type relationship, but the thing that I didn´t realize at the time was that this was mostly my own fault, a response to my own controlling 'masculine' behavior.

Words of wisdom—Recognize when you're not being your true authentic self

If you can relate to any or all of the above, then here's the good news—in 2005, I felt compelled to go on a two specific journeys. My first was to address my health. I attended regular group exercise classes and also worked with two brilliant personal trainers at the gym—Justin Riley and then Chris Stephenson. It took me five years to lose five stone (70 lbs/ 32 kgs) which built up from two half-hour sessions per week to an obsessive 12 hours (too much), and still I plateaued. Even though I hadn't reached my 'normal' target weight, however I knew I looked and felt really good (despite sometimes looking in the mirror and still seeing my old fat self).

My second journey was to specifically seek out the world's leading personal development & relationship experts to heal myself and find out all their secrets & see how they matched with my own years of experiential learning.

I immersed myself in gaining knowledge about the differences between how men & women think, feel, & behave in regard to their personal relationships; also along the way I discovered some very powerful passion & intimacy techniques, strategies, & skills that really work.

These techniques showed me how to heal & love myself, whereas before (with my ex) there was distance, little connection, and the feeling of settling for an 'okay' partnership; I have now reclaimed my true authentic 'feminine' core self, I've learned to let go of control & trust without feeling the need to protect myself in my invisible suit of masculine armor.

I now have a relationship full of red hot passion, intimacy, and massive connection, where I feel alive, loved, & cherished above and beyond my wildest dreams; I've realized this is what I've been craving all my adult life!

I wanted to attract a strong alpha-male who would treat me like a goddess, protect and take care of me, who'd take the lead in a healthy relationship, show me passion, and melt me with his very presence. Wow, on 3rd Jan 2010—I certainly attracted that when I met my soul mate, Paul. So was it all sweetness and light?

Words of wisdom—Knowledge is power

Unfortunately, no, at least not to start with, despite having a very passionate relationship with lots of deep love, intimacy, & connection, every 3-4 weeks we'd end up having big arguments. I couldn't understand why, and after having such a calm peaceful relationship with my ex previously (most likely because he wanted to keep the peace), I knew it must be Paul's fault, right?

Wrong!

Believe it or not, this took me over three years of (sometimes very painful) experiences to learn and finally grasp that the issue of resolving conflicts has a very specific sequence and order. I just needed to learn to handle it in a feminine rather than a masculine way.

Words of wisdom—Challenge is an opportunity to learn and grow

To create calm & intimacy where otherwise there would have been conflict and arguments, I learned that I need to follow a certain sequence to diffuse the situation. For example, if Paul gets irritated or frustrated over something and unfairly takes it out on me (I call this 'lighting the fire'), the temptation for me was to react by adding fuel to the fire, either by getting aggressive (retaliating in anger) becoming defensive (saying 'yes but …'), or justifying (with my 'I'm right' opinion).

Either way, all Paul sees at this point is another male energy challenging his masculinity.

I used to do all of the above on a regular basis, always with the same result. We'd end up having a full-blown major argument. We both used to say things that would be very hurtful & Paul would then withdraw to his 'cave,' sometimes for days at a time and I would feel utterly distraught.

I knew I needed to deal with this by implementing some of the techniques which taught me to respond to him in a feminine way & see my vulnerability as a source of strength (not weakness), which is to pour water on the fire or risk losing our deep connection & intimacy.

The way I pour water on the fire is by letting him see or know that he hurt my feelings with either his words or his body language. I'll respond, for example, by using my forefingers to point playfully at my bottom lip, which I stick out in a little girl sulky pout, complete with big sad puppy dog eyes (which is just one of many 'feminine' responses I use).

He'll then instantly feel guilty for hurting the woman he loves and give himself a far harder time about it than I ever could. The result is that the fire has been put out, intimacy has been maintained, and I can then pick my moment to have my say on the situation in a calm, feminine way.

I'm really excited to say that for many years, peace and calm have prevailed—I know Paul really adores me, and we both now make a conscious effort to deal with potential conflicts in a playful, fun, or calm way. What a relief!

I have personally known what it's like to have suffered the trauma of rape and abuse as a young teenager, in an era when children weren't encouraged to have a voice. I believe I survived these experiences for a reason—to prepare me to inspire women to know they can have a safer, brighter, fulfilling future when it comes to their intimate relationships.

Words of wisdom—Your past does not equal your future (Anthony Robbins)

I specifically help women reclaim their true authentic feminine core selves in the area of intimate relationships. I feel really lucky to have the Ultimate Intimate Soul Mate Relationship. Paul and I have a healthy deep lasting love, passion, and intimacy, with peace & calm and I know that if we can, you can too.

If you're a woman in a relationship and have ever said or thought these words:

I Love My Man But….

- … I still feel unfulfilled

- … We are more like friends than lovers

- … The relationship is lacking passion & intimacy

- … The spark has gone

- … We argue all the time

- … I need more peace & calm in the relationship

- … He's distant most of the time

Or if you're single woman and have ever said or thought these words:

I want a relationship but…

- … There are no good guys out there

- … I always attract losers or players

- … I never get a second date

- … I don't know where start

- … Men don't like powerful / successful women

- … I can't trust men

- … I seem to push men away….

Or whatever else your 'but' is… and you want to know how to 'Reclaim Your Feminine Power' – create/ attract your soulmate relationship and feel fulfilled, fully awakened, & alive?

I'm here, I'm genuinely dedicated to help as many women as possible have the kind of ultimate intimate soul mate relationship they deserve and for which I'm so grateful. I want to share my discoveries & secrets with you. I honestly believe these powerful skills will have a positive impact in reducing divorce, domestic violence, & suicide.

In my FREE report, I share PROVEN techniques that have been tested and that could positively change your current/ future relationship forever—just like I've changed mine & those of thousands of women worldwide.

If you'd like to find out what's in my FREE 'Reclaim Your Feminine Power' report, then go to my website NOW and start your own exciting journey of discovery to lasting love, passion, and intimacy.

***

To Contact Lyn:

www.HunkyCaveman.com

With Love & Big Hugs

Lyn Smith

The Queen of HEARTS

www.HunkyCaveman.com

P.S. I make a difference by helping you make a difference; I have a vision of being able to contribute back on a massive scale. I would love to be involved in leaving a lasting legacy of safety, dignity, and opportunity for children and women who have survived rape, abuse, and severe trauma as a result of war crimes and sex trafficking—through the setting up of a foundation of worldwide 'you can heal your life' centers/ retreats. With the help of people like you reading this book, I know we can do it!

Words of wisdom—ALL'S well in the end and if it isn't well it hasn't ended yet!

Patricia A. Rundblade

Do you know the quality of your conversations will determine your success in life, love, and business?

Author, Speaker, and Transformational Life and Relationship Coach Patricia Rundblade has a passion for all things about life and relationships and being your own hero. In her debut book, *OH FLUX! How Did I Get Here?,* she journeys for the answer to the simplest question about life, "How did I get here?"

Patricia's work and seminars are expertly crafted for people who consider themselves lifelong learners and people of strength who desire to embark on a journey to create healthier and more prosperous relationships in life, love, and business.

Founder of *The Personal Advancement Group*, Patricia shares her innovative ideas and strategies for creating a more purposeful life and building amazing relationships one bold conversation at a time through her signature program "Journey of a Hero: Revealing the Hero Within." She takes her clients on a private journey of discovery, transformation, and creation of their own inner hero. Her philosophy for writing, coaching, and speaking is rooted in the idea of "the conversation is the relationship." While no single conversation guarantees a change, any single conversation can impart change.

Journey of a Hero: Revealing the Hero Within

By Patricia Rundblade

Staring blankly at my time line, I took in the heartbreak and sadness of a life lived in the shadows of detachment. Each event reinforcing the feelings carried for so long; I don't matter, I am alone, and no one will support me. Thinking back, and recalling memories of a life where a vast emptiness existed was filled with the true meaning of being alone and not mattering in the world; especially to my family. What is this I was experiencing and unconscious to?

Continuing to stare at the time line on the table, I had a choice to make. Either continue to be stuck and asleep in my life, or wake up and be conscious of how to be an agent of change for not only myself, but for my children, their children, and future generations. People live in the energy fields of their parents unknowingly. In that moment, the question was "Am I going to continue to allow my life to be defined by this negative energy field, or am I going to be the liberator and shift the cycle of energy for future generations?" Which will you choose?

"OH FLUX! How did I get here?"

Life is amazing! One I would not trade for the world. The amazing life which lay before me was not always this way. About nine years ago, life began the start of a slow implosion with the ending of a 20-year marriage. This young military union showed continual signs of strain from the very beginning and was unknowingly set up for failure. Being in such a dire need of a connection, feeling alone, lonely, unloved, and overlooking many red flags for the sake of what I believed to be true love; optimistically believing with every new base it would get better. A once blossoming flower now dried and wilted in the window of life.

Following hot on the heels of separation and freedom, I jumped headfirst into a post-divorce relationship. This very love-filled relationship lasted four years, and then one day abruptly ended in silence; no more words spoken between us. Confused and in deep pain, emotionally shattered, depressed, and feeling unwanted; often asking myself "Who would want me now?" When reality fully set in with the understanding he actually left without saying another word, I kept asking "What did I do wrong?" Tiny pieces of a destroyed self-esteem and self-confidence littered an already unstable internal floor.

The mask worn to hide the oppressive inner pain among family, friends, and co-workers kept getting tighter with each passing day. Life was stressful, depressing, and unfulfilling. It did not end there. Unable to see the repeated patterns in this life, I decided to move, thinking it would make life better. In 2013, this slow implosion grew to a full on explosion. A series of events transpired and I completely lost who I was as a person in this world. In the course of a few weeks, life was spinning from loss and grief of a dearly loved pet and from the abrupt ending of a revered career in education. An already shattered soul accompanied by a shattered consciousness and an empty blank stare atop the soul-less body walking around each day.

Devastated and feeling like I was living someone else's life, one question kept coming to mind, "Who am I?" Single and sad, children grown and gone, grieving the loss of a beloved pet, my whole identity wrapped up in a career I no longer had, and in debt like most people, the only question rolling through my mind was "How did I get here?"

What a hot mess!

Discovering My Past

While attending my first personal development seminar, reality slapped me in the face. I came to many scary revelations about my life. Revelations that began cracking my steel resolve many times over the course of the weekend. At one point, sitting mouth slightly open, tears rolling down my face, breathing briskly and rapidly as I stared in disbelief at the stage and the man speaking. His words cutting through the unidentified pain in my heart and soul and reaching a depth no one has ever reached before. He spoke of generational pain; naming the pain heavily present upon my shoulders.

Adyashanti describes this type of unconsciousness as generational pain. He states, "Generational pain is a type of pain in the form of a negative energy field traveling down family lines and is passed through generations and generations of unawakened people until someone decides to get conscious enough to start questioning it and wake up from it." A burden I chose to carry unknowingly, and one that left me operating on some pretty heavy negative beliefs about my health, my money, and my life. I was discovering its global impact on my relationship with myself and with others in my life.

You see, up until that weekend, I had no idea generational pain existed. I realized the generational pain lying unconsciously upon my shoulders rooted itself deep in feelings of lack: lack of happiness, love, or money. Creating a limiting belief of "I don't matter in this world" or "I will never be good enough for anyone or anything, and deserving of nothing, including success in my business." My wake-up call from the Universe was loud and noticeable, and in that moment; the moment I was staring at my time line, I woke up. I made the choice to awaken my consciousness and shift the negative energy field tethered to me from generations past.

My life was at stake—I needed to make some serious choices.

When you struggle in your relationships—especially in the one with yourself, that struggle will then be present in your other relationships in life, with love, and with money. I made a decision that this could go on no more—I woke up! As Adyashanti says, "the beauty of releasing this negative energy that is passed on in a family's origin, you become the liberator of that energy—not only for yourself, but for anyone else down the line that it might have gotten passed down to. You become the liberator by seeing that it is not who and what you are and the energy wasn't who or what anybody was—it was just associated because others chose to carry it."

Take a moment and think about your time line. Close your eyes, sit comfortably with your feet firmly planted on the ground, your back straight, head atop your shoulders, your palms face up on your thighs, and taking three deep and cleansing breaths; inhaling and exhaling.

Where do you see your time line in your mind? Is it running through you like a line? Is it behind you? Is it in front of you? How you see your time line has great impact on how you see your past. When you discover how your past has shaped who you are today, then you begin to awaken to the journey laid before you.

Transforming My Present

For the next two years, and through a transformative process of self-evaluation, I came to the realization that the energy field from generational pain did not define me. In reality, it gave me strength. Strength like none I've ever known or experienced. A strength I hungered to share with others who were just like me; those carrying and struggling with an unknown generational pain. In working with clients, as they journey on the discovery of their own inner hero, they come to awaken from the generational dream state that has them stuck and trapped.

Ask yourself, "how are you showing up in your life?"

Are you awake or unconsciously moving through each day unaware?

As I became more awakened and present to this life laid before me, the path littered with multiple layers of emotional abandonment and feelings of rejection began to fall away. These patterns have been repeating themselves through my lifetime from early childhood through marriage, in dating relationships, and even more evident in business and with attracting clients.

The main result of this revelation, and from evaluation of my experiences, I discovered a hero; the hero within me. A hero like no other designed for me by the Divine and standing true in the power of relationships. This innate ability to navigate and build healthy relationships is designed to bring abundance and prosperity to my life, and to many others on so many levels each and every day. You see, throughout my journey, I realized I was the only hero in and for my life.

What defines a Hero? When you look at Greek Mythology, Hero is identified as a warrior who when in danger and adversity demonstrated traits of courage, self-sacrifice, and bravery, and is boldly admired for his qualities of nobility. The most notable Greek Hero is Hector and is most widely known for his peace-loving nature, for being bold, yet thoughtful, and displaying courage and bravery when the developing world was in chaos and turmoil.

What defines you as a Hero? How do you define your inner Hero? When your world is in turmoil and chaos, what are the traits you demonstrate to return your battlefield to inner peace and awareness?

Along this Journey of a Hero, you begin to unravel the chaos and turmoil of your inner battlefield where you approach the threshold of transformation. Revelations and discoveries of who you became and the true you waiting to be revealed begin to unfold. Every step of this journey challenging your precepts and paradigms, causing you to ask, "How did I get here?"

I'll ask you again, "how are you showing up in your life?"

Transforming my reality of who I am in this world, and defining how I show up in this life has strengthened my desire to share this with others. To serve as many people as I can in creating a healing of generational pain, generating harmony in building healthy relationships, and change the trajectory of humanity toward greater peace one deeply bold conversation at a time.

Our ability to understand our world, and the experiences in it is achieved through three main areas such as how we conceptualize our experiences through our senses, through the behaviors we demonstrate, and the power of our words.

By transforming your previously written imprints you currently use as the guidelines to process the experiences in your life, the battlefield of turmoil and chaos becomes inner peace and awareness. When you are in alignment with what you think, what you feel, and what you say, then you are truly living in the power and essence of your inner hero.

Creating Your Dreams

Creating the life you envision begins by changing the conversations you have with others and yourself. The verbal and non-verbal language we use to understand our experiences and all the signals we received from others are taken in and given meaning and codes for future experiences. Truthfully, many of us are operating with outdated codes.

The maps we use to process an experience is run through a set of paradigms from old experiences and many times do not reflect our current thinking. Often leaving you to feel confused as to why the outcome was different than what you thought it would be. When you create updated or new codes of processing, then you are able to create a specific and desired result. In order for true transformation to happen, it has to occur on all levels in your life.

Crafting the words necessary to shape how you speak also shapes how you are seen because the words you choose will have power to create. You will speak into existence the life you have envisioned time and time again. Once you begin to speak the power of your words, your body will follow. You will feel the full meaning of your words in every cell and generating the actions and behaviors, giving strength to your inner hero. Thus generating emotional strength with each movement and solidifying a quiet inner foundation.

The #1 result my clients say they experience when on their own Journey of a Hero: Revealing the Hero Within is discovering the power they hold within:

To champion confidence and inner strength for greater levels of trust and success

To relax into healthier relationships by making poor relationships better, and good relationships great.

To create empowered conversations and relationships in life for greater love and in business for maximized profitability.

To understand and design their own relationship blueprint for the life they envision

Once you discover how your past has shaped who you are as a person, then you can begin the process of transforming your present to create the future you have envisioned. Living a life of passion, fulfillment, and authenticity; living your Hero Power and revealing the Hero within.

***

To Contact Patricia:

Join me on this amazing journey of discovery. Patricia's dedication to personal development and growth is shared with others in bi-monthly discussion groups, seminars, workshops, and trainings. For more information about Patricia, check out her website. Download your free gift and subscribe to her monthly newsletter, *"Letters From the Heart"* filled with helpful and transformational information to help you continue to grow along your journey of self-discovery.

Friend me on Facebook @ facebook.com/PatriciaRundblade

Connect with me on LinkedIn @ www.linkedin.com/pub/patricia-rundblade/16/449/596

Tweet with me on Twitter @ twitter.com/1CoachPatsy

Visit my website The Personal Advancement Group

Need a Speaker? Check me out here San Diego Speakers Guild

Watch a video of me on YouTube at Patricia Rundblade

Read with me on my Blog at OHFLUX @ coachpatsy.tumblr.com

Email me at patricia@patriciarundblade.com

Call me at (661) 209-2172

Peggy Sealfon

Peggy Sealfon is a Personal Development Coach and Motivational Speaker who helps clients overcome stress, anxiety, trauma and pain to live happy, abundant, fearless lives. Her _Integrated Life Personal Coaching System_ is a customized fast-track approach to awaken personal balance and ignite the inner source of empowerment.

Peggy is described as "extraordinary," "a calming spirit," "crackling with vitality, intelligence and warmth" and "she inspires others." Certified in life-changing modalities from ancient yogic techniques, mindfulness, and spirituality to training in modern psychology, energy medicine, and the neurosciences, Peggy intuitively formulates effective protocols for individuals facing challenges ranging from health to relationships, work, finances, and life purpose. She assists clients around the world towards higher levels of physical, mental, and emotional well-being using a highly advanced interactive approach.

Peggy also works with companies to create cutting-edge programs for improving productivity of employees and corporate teams. Her book *Escape From Anxiety—Supercharge Your Life With Powerful Strategies From A to Z* is a professional and personal compilation of effective, transformational techniques (available at Amazon, Barnes & Noble, or EscapeFromAnxiety.com). Originally from New York City, Peggy currently resides in southwest Florida.

An Integrated Life Is the Way to Authentic Success

By Peggy Sealfon

Success is relative and may not be what you imagine. Robert was certain he would have the perfect life once he had accumulated millions of dollars. Ironically, after persistent hard work when he realized his dream, instead of basking in the rewards of his determination, he became anxious managing his new homes, an exotic car collection, and watching over his investments. He feared losing everything in a flash of economic catastrophe. His exaggerated worries were making him physically sick. He couldn't appreciate his acquisitions or enjoy quality time with his devoted wife and three beautiful daughters.

His intense anxiety is not all that different from another client who could barely pay her bills. Stella faced spiraling health costs after an accident left her unable to work. Her loving husband and grown son were very supportive, but she felt useless, overwhelmed, and depressed.

Work and money are often associated with success, fueled by the perception that you are what you do. The myth is that the more money you have, the better and more significant you feel. According to several studies, it simply isn't true. A 30-percent increase in salary does not equal 30-percent more happiness. Yet wage earners strive to grow their salaries. A multi-millionaire wants to become a billionaire.

Human nature drives us to seek perpetual improvement. We're always working towards bettering our situation, which can be positive. Learning to be resilient, confident, and able to deal with constant change is critical to our very evolution. But adapting to change can be tough.

In retrospect, my own path is a veritable study in change. I have a PhD in reinventing myself and a Master's degree in fearlessness. My career followed a circuitous road of constantly changing interests and circumstances. I started as a freelance journalist in New York City writing for the *New York Times, Newsweek International*, and other publications. I then launched a couple of specialty retail stores and eventually opened my own advertising agency. All along the way, I trained in stress-relieving and wellness modalities for personal survival (which eventually became my life work). I did each business capably, but inwardly I struggled with insecurity.

As far back as I remember, I was a workaholic, an adrenaline junkie. I perceived these as desirable traits of successful people. I believed that if something wasn't working, I had to work harder to make it happen. I catapulted myself into projects without taking time to eat or sleep. In my mind, I was accomplishing great things and on my way to making huge fortunes. If I stopped, I could lose momentum and end up a total failure. My thinking was distorted.

From today's vantage point, I understand that I had not developed integration where mind and body align to ignite the infinite inner power that burns with purpose and clarity. My behavior was unsustainable on a relentless seesaw. I shifted from productive highs, feeling motivated and passionate, to plummeting to the depths of fear, pain, and illnesses, feeling hopeless. I was stuck in a destructive cycle. I was stressed and did not know how to stop.

Chronic stress is pandemic and another lifestyle liability. It is killing us one by one and costing companies billions of dollars. A little stress is good. If someone is about to step on stage to address hundreds of his peers, stress can release enough adrenaline to keep him focused, sharp, and more energized. But acute stress can be a life wrecker. For Robert, stress severely undermined his ability to function, ruined his relationships, and critically damaged his health. Unfortunately, in our chaotic, fast-paced world, we accept stress as normal. Symptoms such as irritability, impatience, bad behavior, fatigue, nervousness, and poor performance often get casually dismissed. We ignore the telltale signs while going at full force until we can't go anymore, finally hitting bottom and breaking down. Robert suffered a stroke.

Years ago, I taught a "Sports Performance Workshop" at a Florida resort. I offered easy methods for tennis players to improve their games. One technique is an Integrative Relaxation experience, a guided journey into deep levels of relaxation based on an ancient yogic method called *Yoga Nidra*. In this activity, participants often reach levels of consciousness approaching alpha and even theta states, which mimic the benefits of sleep. Scientific studies show that just 20 minutes is equivalent to the restorative effects of three to four hours of deep REM (rapid eye movement) sleep. It quickly improves muscle recovery and so much more.

After the session, a gray-haired gentleman in his mid-50s with peaceful-looking eyes approached me. He confessed that he had never felt *that* relaxed in his entire life. A shocking revelation! In almost six decades, Joe had never allowed himself to let go and truly relax. Throughout his life, he suffered painful joints and a variety of other dismissible illnesses. Then serious trauma hit a few years earlier when an incapacitating heart attack forced him into early retirement. As we talked, Joe had an epiphany, realizing that he was always trying to control everything in his life, which put him under constant tension. Stress had taken its toll.

In another experience, a high-driving middle-aged corporate executive came to one of my "Integrated Life" programs. At the end of the first session, he asked in an almost accusing voice if I'd changed the lighting in the room. "Why?" I questioned. "When I first came in, it looked really dark and dingy," he paused to scan the room slowly as if he was viewing it for the first time. Then he gushed: "Now it's beautiful. Really beautiful." Nothing in the room had changed. In a span of 90 minutes, *he* had changed. He had deeply relaxed and, in so doing, his perceptions were altered. He let go of burdens and was able to *see* differently. It's a powerful transition and has roots in our biology, especially in our "fight or flight" response.

The laws of nature propel us biologically into a perfect state of homeostasis that normally optimize body and mind to reach the most efficient levels. But when we're anxious, exhausted, and out of alignment for long periods, the stress response keeps us dangerously in high alert. Designed for our survival, these stress hormones were meant to be released only for brief spurts to give us the strength to fight or run away from the predator. When they flow constantly, our immune system gets overwhelmed and our mind becomes dull and unfocused. So how do we shift from survive to thrive?

Over decades of advanced studies in the science and system of human development, I acquired a deep understanding about the benefits of achieving an integrated life. With constant practice, I transformed my own dysfunctional existence and now assist others. True realization in life is about awakening to personal balance and *presentness*. It is the integration of the physical, mental, and emotional aspects of our being which influence our relationships, work, play, health, finances, and especially finding life's purpose.

Authentic success is the ability to live courageously in this very moment, fully engaged and accept what *is* without deferring satisfaction to some future point. Recognizing your own expansiveness in this millisecond opens the connection to your intuition. The process allows you to be better guided in reaching an equilibrium of *knowingness*, contentment, and pleasure. As a perpetual work in progress, you're continually evolving towards better versions of yourself. Though perhaps unaware, you're experimenting with ways to bring all facets into harmony and when that happens, you feel good. But for most people, the experience is fleeting. Many do not know how to consciously enter into that place of bliss. Living an integrated life is the formula for happiness and happiness is the ultimate success.

Everyone is capable of mastering the inner game, but not everyone takes the time to comprehend the methodology. It is a training that brings body and mind into ecstatic balance as a viable solution to neutralize today's overwhelming challenges. It was the way I leveled my manic seesaw. I learned techniques to release all struggles and embrace a more effective and effortless lifestyle that is naturally channeled from within. The process—which is ongoing—allows me to stay peaceful and centered. Even in the face of enormous crises, I can function consistently at peak levels with little stress.

The method isn't about working harder or making more money (although abundance may be the outcome). But it's working from a place of calmness to live more generously from the source of your own power and purpose. The result is that you have infinite energy, balanced health, and you see solutions where before you may have only seen problems. The techniques you may personally need may range from physical to metaphysical, psychological to spiritual.

To assist you on your journey of self-empowerment, consider a few introductory steps to light the way to a more integrated state of being. Allow yourself to be vulnerable as you explore and accept who you are in the divine dimension of infinite possibilities.

SELF-ASSESSMENT & SELF-AWARENESS

Choose a quiet place, free of distractions, and take a few minutes to reflect on yourself and your current situation. Identify one area in which you face difficulties. Where are you feeling out of balance? Is it your health? Finances? Relationships? Notice what is top-of-mind and write your perceptions in a few sentences. There is always one part of life that needs your attention. If your relationship is fabulous, then work may suffer or vice versa. Be specific, uninhibited, and honest.

When you're done writing, notice words you've used to describe your condition. Is there self-criticism in your comment? This method allows you to sharpen an internal awareness of your true self. It is vital to start with where you are and face your fears.

Your mental chatter has a huge impact on how you perceive your reality and also how you respond to the external world. The seeds of self-talk are often planted in childhood by parents, teachers, or even friends who thoughtlessly exclaim something like "Oh you'll never amount to anything." Such concepts take root in your core and influence many of your choices throughout life. You may feel undeserving or that you're just not good enough. You may compare yourself to others or are afraid of being judged. When you take time to notice what you're thinking, you enter a more mindful place, which is the first step to personal growth and inner truth.

The *Law of Attraction* contends that "like attracts like." In *The Science of Getting Rich*, a brilliant book published in 1910, author Wallace D. Wattles reveals that by believing in the object of your desire and focusing thoughts on it will lead to that object or goal being realized on the material plane. (Wattles' concept is the central point of *The Secret*.)

Simply stated, negative thinking attracts negative results. Positive thinking manifests positive results. Rather than science, Wattles attributes his premise to the viewpoint that God is pervasive and can deliver whatever you focus on. You may consider it God, faith, *Prana,* Holy Spirit, *Qi,* universal cosmic powers, divine love, or energy. What matters is having awareness about *what is* on all the subtle energetic levels so that you can let go of *what is not*. This is especially important if you are unconsciously exacerbating negative thinking, which saps your strengths, fragments energies, and devastates your well-being.

In cellular biology and neurosciences, it is now understood that genes turn on or off by various signals from emotions, thoughts, and feelings. Therefore, your very thoughts control your biology. Change your thinking and you change how your body functions and influence more desirable adjustments in areas of your life that seem troubled.

Let's dig deeper. This energetic exchange moves between subatomic particles within our bodies, minds, and even our universe. The body is an energetic field filled with patterns of information with the heart at the center. Electrical, magnetic, light, and electromagnetic signals travel from the heart to the brain, where the input is appropriately disseminated, activating responses in our physical body. There's an innate intelligence in the body to maintain self-regulation, but we now know that emotions can have an enormous influence and cause us to flip out of alignment.

This basic energetic system is not bound by time or space. It is a living, moving force. Everything under the sun (and including the sun) has an energy pulse, a vibrational frequency. We are like transmitters and receivers responding and reacting to all elements in our field of energy or consciousness, not only from within, but from outside. Inside we're flooded with emotions and thoughts. Outside we're exposed to electromagnetic frequencies from our grid systems. These are all part of a massive energy field which we feel on subtle levels. The more we tune in to our essential natures, the more we can stay in an integrated, more effortless state.

CREATE POSITIVE CHANGE

In the self-assessment exercise, you observed stories from a conflicted part of your life. These views are recordings from your past, resurfacing in the present. They are beliefs, but not necessarily true. (Remember that humans once believed the world was flat!) When external triggers occur, neurons in your brain—which are wired together in your memory—are activated to replay the same old scenarios. These negative neural pathways become grooved into habitual cycles of responses that can harm your spirit and hold you back from your personal potential for success.

The good news is that you can interrupt these patterns by mindfully observing any destructive thought or emotion and replacing it with a positive expression. So once you become aware of unproductive self-talk and emotional reactions, you can create fundamental change. Here are examples of healthy statements to use as an "interrupter" to switch your focus from a bad reaction to a good response (or create your own constructive phrases):

- I'm healthy, happy, and filled with love.
- I'm smart, capable, focused and calm.
- I love myself and accept myself as I am.
- I embrace and learn from all experiences of life unconditionally.

Every time you notice an adverse reaction whether to a situation or person—choose one phrase to repeat over and over. The more you use a productive affirmation, the more it conditions your mind to be optimistic and that thought—along with associated emotional signals— delivers a productive effect on your body and becomes permanently stored in your memory.

Let me share a simplistic example of how the strategy worked for me. I was playing a singles' tennis match for a USTA (United States Tennis Association) team. The match was on red clay under lights and my opponent was left-handed and 20 years my junior. I thought: "I hate all of this. I hate nighttime tennis. I can't do this. I'm no good. I shouldn't have accepted to play this match."

I was playing horribly until after a few games I recognized how badly I was abusing myself with my incessant rants. Immediately, I changed my focus, repeating: "I'm a person of great value. I'm an expression of the divine." I instantly felt energized and started playing better. The match continued for three long hours and, in the end, I won! The affirmation filled me with energy, changed my brain waves, transformed my beliefs, and gave my body a chance to perform at a higher level. Words and expressions are powerful.

Both clients Robert and Stella—while at very different financial levels and situations—learned to use self-awareness and mindfulness along with other integrated strategies to influence long-term positive changes in their attitudes, health, and well-being. With supportive coaching, they regularly reviewed priorities and evaluated aspects of utmost importance, particularly valuing their personal purpose and special people in their lives.

One particularly helpful technique that both incorporated immediately has been to take regular time-outs from tasks, responsibilities, and even from worries to shift out of stress. These pauses are reminders to observe and appreciate who they are and be grateful for what they have. Each has discovered that the transformational journey to inner certainty takes practice and has become extremely valuable. They both feel more vital and alive.

A KEY STEP

You can do the same by committing to take daily breaks. Allocate a few minutes every day to enter a place of calmness. Stretch and take a few slow deep breaths. Enjoy what I call a *productivity pause* and drop into a relaxed, meditative state. (Access and use my free audio 3MinutestoDestress.com) The spacious silence is a profound place to reconnect to your intuition, creativity, and your life force. It will rekindle your energies and awaken your mind and spirit.

Imagine if you lost $100 today, would you still be you? How about losing $10,000, would you still be here? What would you be thinking about yourself? You are not your bank account, your job,

Insights into Self-Empowerment

your wardrobe, your health, or even your thoughts. You are so much more expansive, an infinite energy being full of light, love, and unmanifested potential.

Breathe deeply, dance wildly, sing to the sparrows, or indulge in hilarious laughter and then pause to observe what you want to change in your life. Practice the strategies in this chapter. They will reveal that you are significant, whole, and complete as you are. Once you quiet the disturbances of the mind and connect to the innate knowledge within, you'll produce more with less effort. You'll release conflicts of the ego about self-worth. You'll heal your body and discover your path. You will know your purpose and enter a heavenly place of integration. Let go of self-doubts as you step into absolute confidence and accept your greatness.

As Abraham Lincoln once said: "In the end, it's not the years in your life that count. It's the life in your years." Seize opportunities and create your new destiny of fulfilment and genuine happiness. The remarkable world of authentic success awaits you.

***

To contact Peggy:

Peggy@PeggySealfon.com

www.PeggySealfon.com

Facebook: www.facebook.com/peggysealfon.personaldevelopmentcoach

Twitter: https://twitter.com/StonewaterSt

LinkedIn: https://www.linkedin.com/in/peggysealfon

Instagram: https://instagram.com/peggysealfon/

Paul Lowe

Paul was born on the 25th October 1960 in an inner-city part of Nottingham, England. As an only child, he was influenced in his formative years by the love of his mother and grandmother; his parents split up when he was aged three. Despite his humble existence, Paul was happy.

However, from the age of eight, his life became one stark polarization of darkness and light for over four decades. An alcohol addiction and a violent up-bringing ensured Paul's world was in constant turmoil; although academic achievement and having three beautiful kids significantly challenged the darkness.

It was during the decade of concentrated education that Paul became conscious of his personal development journey; a first degree in Education was then followed by a Masters in Customer Service & Quality Management; the latter influenced by eminent practitioners such as Covey, Deming, and Peters, to name but three.

More vocationally, Paul is a qualified ILM level-5 business coach and he now uses his extremely diverse life experiences to make a positive impact on the lives of individuals and communities—globally. As the founder of the HEARTS not-for-profit brand, he is totally committed to the HEARTS acronym of: **Helping Everyone Achieve Results Towards Success**

From Forest Wilderness to Global Contribution

By Paul Lowe

Introduction

At the turn of the millennium, I self-published a book—called the *Game of Life*—that was an autobiographical account of my challenging journey during the first 40 years of my life.

Although poorly written, let this not masquerade the substance it contained and more importantly, the foundation it provided to pen these words; a chapter that will hopefully provide at least a modicum of inspiration to those who choose to read it.

I recall once reading somewhere the notion that our lives break naturally into two halves, with 'half-time' coming somewhere between the ages of thirty and fifty years old. As I remember, the first-half is all about getting & gaining and living for the moment in the tangible here-and-now.

The second-half is generally more risky because it has to do with searching for something more rewarding and meaningful than the results of our first-half efforts; it involves delving into the unknown—in essence, taking a leap of faith.

However, my personal story does not reflect that kind of idealism; but rather an account of a life acutely dominated by addiction, violence, and a very dark existence—sandwiching the odd moments of joy—all combining to create many years of confusion.

From Happiness To Hell

I was born at the start of the Swinging Sixties and—after my parents split up when I was three—my mother and I moved to an inner-city council area called Bestwood Estate to live with my grandmother Winnie.

Although we were extremely poor, I recall fond memories of those impoverished days; until the age of about seven that is. That's when my mother started seeing a man that lived next door to us and—a year later—ended up marrying him in 1968.

As much as I remember the formative years of my life with pride and happiness—nostalgically reflecting upon a golden era for music and football—I'm equally polarized in my recollections of how this new guy's despicable and destructive behavior changed my life for the worse.

Initially starting out with simple acts of mental cruelty towards my mother and me, he then progressed on to spates of violence towards us both; this beast undoubtedly turned out to be one of the vilest pieces of crap it has ever been my misfortune to come across.

As a result of this marriage, we had to uproot from my beloved Bestwood and move the other side of Nottingham—to the countryside—and for a city boy like me, it was a living hell. All the love and certainty had been removed from my world and I felt so desperate and sad.

Everything I had ever known and loved had been taken away from me—contact with my grandma Winnie; my passion for listening to music and—above all—the dream that maybe one day I would represent Nottingham Forest Football Club.

My whole existence had become an unstable mess almost overnight. The new country-boy kids didn't like football and the beast deliberately deprived me of these two fervent passions in my life.

The Change[9]

This acute loss lasted for two long, distressing years until my exile was temporarily over. I can still recall the elation—at the tender age of almost 10—when my mother told me she was leaving him.

In September 1970, I returned for the final year at my old Junior School—and passed my 11+ exam, which gained me a place at the nearby Grammar School. I was now back home and free to enjoy my music and Nottingham Forest FC; life was blissfully good once again.

However, this euphoria turned out to be short-lived on several accounts. Firstly, I had begun to feel insecure and depressed because of the cruelty my mother and I painfully suffered from the beast; this had scarred me more badly than I realized, and the legacy was to live on for years.

Secondly, football was banned from being played at Grammar School; it had a steeped tradition of playing rugby and any mention of football was frowned upon by the (mostly) Victorian-style masters presiding over us.

However, if these two aspects were to cause me distress, this was nothing compared to what transpired later. Within a few weeks, my mother was re-united with the beast and once again, my world was shattered; this marking the start of another three torturous years.

All his previous promises of change and happiness soon disappeared and the violence and heartlessness soon returned with a vengeance—and all this when I was still barely eleven years old. I tried running away from home a couple of times and nervously slept rough on the nearby common.

My only salvation through this living hell was the belief that I would one day be playing for my beloved Forest; this obsession being challenged by a newfound mechanism—the demon drink! My mother was a secret drinker and by the age of 12, I was regularly helping myself to tots from her stashes of sherry & whisky.

This only compounded the situation and I attempted suicide at 13; I was at my breaking point and all my ever-growing instincts for survival were severely being tested to the limit. By now, the violence I was experiencing at the hands of the beast was having a dramatic knock-on effect to me.

This was 'fight-or-flight' and I was determined not to fly again! I somehow had the faith to accept there was a reason for this test. If I was experiencing this heartache, surely others would be too; and I was prepared to fight for them as well—consciously accepting my life now had purpose!

Struggling To Survive

Such was my anguish at home that I was now creating a diversionary tactic; I was developing another character—one that would allow me to escape and become somebody else; a facade that was perceived by others as me being a no-nonsense hard-nut—not caring about anyone or anything.

By the time I was barely 16, my passion for music was becoming irrelevant, and being replaced by the call to fight for others. This—along with my love for Forest—had given me a strong sense of identity and purpose.

My intensity towards Forest was beyond most people's comprehension, even the vast majority of the football crazy kids I grew up with on Bestwood. Looking back, it was a manifestation of an all-or-nothing mindset. There was no grey in-between.

Forest gave me an identity at a time when—through my turbulent childhood—I had effectively lost my own. By now, I also found myself being strongly drawn towards the Irish fraternities; regularly visiting the allotments (caves) of the men-folk on Sunday mornings for a nip or two of Potcheen and tales of bare-knuckle fighting.

The Change[9]

Although I was naturally a loving, caring, and sensitive type of child, I had found myself developing a safety mechanism that kept people at arm's length; this front was displayed by being aggressive and confrontational—in effect, I was living a massive lie.

Consequently—in November 1974—things were about to come to a head and change forever; after being kept behind at school for a detention, I knew that returning home late that night would mean big trouble.

I began trembling with anticipation as I sprinted home with all the adrenaline and nervous energy of a hunted gazelle. As I entered the back door, the inevitable happened; the beast attacked me incessantly. I somehow weathered the onslaught and wiped the streams of crimson blood from my face.

As I did so, I managed to catch sight of a bread knife on the kitchen table; I lunged for it and took my stance with only one thought in mind, and it wasn't to cut bread!

The hunted had now become the hunter; my temper was so fierce, like a caged and tormented tiger. The winds of change were blowing and this was the first time I became conscious of control. Like all bullies when threatened with their own treatment, he cowered away.

The anticipated sequel having not materialized, my mother and me simply packed our bags and left with me vowing to the beast that one day I would return and gain my revenge.

This proved to be a significant turning point in my life; because of all the emotional pain I had suffered over the previous few years, I now found myself more than ever becoming alcohol dependent; whilst—at the same time—becoming embroiled in constant conflict and fights.

As I progressed beyond my teens, one of the lowest points of my life occurred on New Year's Eve 1982, with the news that my Grandma

Winnie had died. As an 'old-school' matriarch, she was so resilient, strong, and was as solid and tough as a majestic oak tree.

After Winnie's death, to say I waged war on society would be a massive understatement. I took it upon myself to be judge, jury, and executioner towards any Tom, Dick, or Harry that I perceived was a bully; I was a rebel with a cause!

For a while, sheer willpower and determination saw me turn things around. At the age of 23, I got married and by 28, had three beautiful kids; as well as having a lovely home and a good job too. But after a while, the cracks started to reappear and I started drinking heavily again; the demon drink had me firmly in its clutches.

In 1988—some 14 years on—I reached rock-bottom in my life; I split up from my wife and kids and began to drift into complete oblivion. Like all heavy drinkers, my thought processes had become badly distorted and I couldn't rid myself of the memories relating to the previous torture and abuse.

At this point, I finally confronted the beast; 20 years of hatred had been allowed to fester and—in my emotionally-twisted logic—it was now time to redress the balance for all the anguish and pain he'd caused. I'd constantly re-lived every slap, punch, and sadistic act he'd delivered to my mother and me.

The upshot was I intended to kill him, but—after setting about my 'duty'—the universe intervened and my intention was not fulfilled; with both our lives being spared—his from death and mine from serving a life sentence in prison.

Searching & Learning

Coming so close to totally ruining my life instigated another 'dry-run.' I was re-united with my family; I got a good job and was starting to do what I'd long-since been conscious of being put on this earth to do—help others. However, my significant fund-raising exploits would always be tested by heavy drinking binges.

Subsequently becoming unemployed in 1991, I decided to embark upon a long phase of learning—spanning over a decade—that resulted in me achieving a teaching degree and Master's degree; my studies fitting-in around disciplined periods of abstinence, before inevitably reverting to wild benders!

More important than the academic achievement was the process of continuous improvement I resonated with. In retrospect, this philosophy was instrumental in laying the foundations for my personal development journey; I was greatly inspired by the prospect of being the best I could be and then, serving others.

Whilst this was an admirable focus, I was still dealing with my own demons; my views were still very polarized—life was either black or white and I rarely showed any flexibility, especially in matters of potential conflict; I would be judge, jury, and executioner and ask questions later!

Irrespective, I look back on the last 20-odd years or so of what lessons I have learnt and how these can be passed-on for the benefit of others. Lessons—not in an academic sense—but in a real practical life-improving way; put simply, I don't want people to learn the hard way, like me.

Therefore, after careful reflection, I have chosen some pertinent things I would love to have been taught at a very early age: 7 Key Lessons to Change Your Life!

1. Past – the way forward

I spent many years dwelling on the past and letting those negativities influence what may happen in the future. In releasing the past, you take back your own power; and focus on what you want now—instead of concentrating on what you don't want.

2. Change – become the best you can be

Continuing the Forest theme, I realize that my happiness was dependent upon Forest's results—I was powerless! You assume control by creating your own effective acorn DNA and growing into a majestic oak, serving life's universal forests.

3. Love – starts with the Self first

Because my inner-world was in complete turmoil, I looked for external validation in all my relationships. If you take responsibility for creating self-love, forgiveness, and gratitude, the ego will be prevented from ruling your world and creating chaos.

4. Forgiveness – learning to let go

Because of my survival conditioning, my ego became all-important; acting as a shield against vulnerability. By embracing that self-acceptance and self-approval will positively change your life, the ego will be overshadowed by the Self.

5. Gratitude – is a wonderful attitude

Arguably, the most powerful lesson I've learned is the power of gratitude. By learning to let go and showing vulnerability, you can make sense of your past; manifesting inner peace and creating a powerful vision statement for the future.

6. GAME – constantly raising the bar

In my early years' struggles, I looked externally to Forest's results for my hope and inspiration rather than searching within. You can improve your GAME by embracing things daily that serve you such as Gratitude, Affirmations, Meditation, & Exercise.

7. Prosperity – overcome limiting beliefs

I was conditioned with so many limiting beliefs—particularly around deservedness—that it was impossible to progress. To prosper, you need to commit to your own well-being first before contributing to others; you cannot give what you do not have!

Contributing Hearts

The breakthrough in my constant progress-sabotage cycle appeared after an almighty binging session. On February 7th February 2010, I barely awoke from a drunken stupor with the realization I was going to die—I knew my time had come!

Throughout the following critical days, I somehow mustered the awareness to know that life would be very different if I survived; I did and to this day, I haven't touched a drop since.

Having stared death in the face, everything I now feel strongly reaffirms that the time for my emergence is definitely here. Having been very confused for the majority of my life about my identity and what my true soul's purpose is, my vision statement now offers clarity:

> **As an author, Contribution Coach, and social investor, I perform on the Stage of Life for the betterment of humanity; with no curtain between back and front—my roles are congruent.**
>
> **Backstage, my vocation as a coach enables me to reach out to people world-wide—fulfilling my passion of serving others—as I continue to emerge through life's scenes.**
>
> **Front stage, I facilitate contributing HEARTS—*Helping Everyone Achieve Results Towards Success*—so we may all play our part in creating mutually-beneficial global communities.**

Even in my darkest hours, I had a sense of purpose—albeit vague—that has continued to grow over the decades. Today, my awareness manifests itself in the work I do both as a coach and also through the charity & community projects I'm involved in.

All my life, I've always committed to making a positive difference in others' lives; none more so since the formation of the HEARTS community-enhancing entities—offering global support & local benefits.

HEARTS Global CIC is totally focused and committed to making a powerful, positive difference to communities—locally, nationally, and globally; achieved by two different ways.

Firstly, by providing a range of core services that add outstanding value to individuals and communities; and secondly, by re-investing profits back into educational, life-improving projects.

Also, its sister organization—the Sporting HEARTS charity—provides a sporting chance in life to young people from disadvantaged communities within the UK; since 2010, it has already positively affected the lives of over 3,000 young people.

With the second-half of my life underway, I recognize that all those years in 'dark soil' was merely a planting exercise, ready for when this particular acorn was ready to transform into a solid oak; making significant contributions to universal forests.

As I reflect upon the many relationships within my first-half, there were few, if any, that were more influential than the one with the demon drink. So much so, that I previously penned a poem—subsequently published—about its destructive powers.

A Question of Bottle

A man in his prison cell, all alone and he's down;

His eyes are all bloodshot and his face wears a frown.

The Change[9]

In one form or another a life behind bars;

He once had it all, fast money – fast cars.

But now he is broken and everything is lost;

The legacy of booze, was it all worth the cost?

He needed his tipple to help him get by;

Now everything is lost, he wished he'd stayed dry.

The drink was a comfort when things got too tough;

At night he felt numb, in the morning just rough.

The lies and the violence he promised would cease;

But booze had control and never gave peace.

Tears stroke his cheeks as he thinks of it now;

Perhaps he will change, if only he knew how?

It's a question of bottle and which one to choose;

The one full of guts, or the one full of booze.

Neither is easy and both promise gains;

But one offers hope, the other just pains.

So when you're alone with only booze as your friend;

Find a new way of being – it's better in the end.

As this story concludes, I offer my lifetime message –

7 Simple Words to Change Your Life Forever:

One Chapter Doesn't Define Your Story – Contribute!

***

To Contact Paul:

To learn more about the life-enhancing work of Paul and HEARTS, please visit:

www.paul-lowe.org

www.heartsglobal.org www.sportinghearts.org.uk

Pennie Quaile-Pearce

SRN, MSc, LCH, RMA, Cert Ed.

Pennie is CEO of Acorn to Oak, the International School of Energy Medicine. Her role is to keep the vibration of Acorn to Oak at the highest and most pure. To strategically head the development team and grow Acorn to Oak onto a more prominent national and international stage. Her experience encompasses over 20 years in the field of orthodox medicine, specializing in trauma and intensive care, it also includes work with the Red Cross and International Voluntary Services (IVS). In 1992, she retrained as a Homoeopath. In 1994, as a Reiki Master/Teacher. In 1996, a Bodhisoul® Breathwork Practitioner. She later went on to write and introduce Breath4Life™ Breath Work into the UK, in 2005 the first set of Breath4Life™ Breath Work Practitioner were trained. She is also a Life, Love, and Spiritual coach/guide, Spiritual Response Therapist. A trained teacher, who specialized in course creation and development. Clients call Pennie a 'spiritual midwife.' Pennie calls herself a 'divine waitress.' She is all of these things and a spiritual entrepreneur.

Breathe The Change

Pennie Quaile-Pearce

If we don't go within, we go without

In this chapter, I discuss the process of self-healing and breath. How we go from not knowing what to do, to beginning to realize that if we don't go within, we go without.

Driving in my car a few weeks ago, listening to the local radio, they made an announcement: "Due to the economic climate, we need to let you know the light at the end of the tunnel has been switched off!" I grinned at the humor of the announcer, but thought, *"Wow, it's amazing how people believe we are all suffering from a lack of resources."* It raises many questions.

Taking control - who can we believe and trust?

There are so many books, e-books, articles, and magazines covering alternative and complementary therapies. New age this, new age that. Health and fitness gurus, spiritual gurus, even management gurus. Men are from Mars and Women are from Venus. Experts telling you up is down and down is up. Being encouraged to get in touch with your inner child, adult, grandparent, German Shepherd? Festivals of mind, body, and spirit. Holistic living. Healing arts. It's enough to confuse a saint, let alone an average person. What do you read? Who can you believe and trust? Are these gurus for real or just plain weird?

How do we proceed if we are looking for answers?

How do we know that the therapist or workshop leader is trustworthy and not just there to take our money and run? Are these workshops just plain entertainment value and of no practical use for self-healing or personal growth? What or who will help us find the answers we need?

Are these some of the thoughts that crowd your mind? Well they have mine.

If we ask for help then it will appear

I have found that the answers to our questions all come from within ourselves. You know what will suit you best if you listen to the quiet and insistent voice from within. Not the voice that beats us up saying that we're not worth it, or that no one and nothing can help us in the situation we find ourselves. If we quietly ask for help, then it will appear in some guise or another.

Recognizing the help

There is a wonderful story of a man in a flood. The man wakes one morning to find that the river near his house has burst its banks and the water has invaded the ground floor of his house. Not too worried about this, he moves to the first floor, but the water level keeps on rising. He has to climb onto the roof where he watches the water level rise higher and higher. He realizes that he is now in some danger and prays to God to save him. He sees a boat which stops and the occupant shouts to get aboard. He replies "No, don't worry about me, God will save me." He sits and waits. A helicopter flies by and lets down a rope, but his answer is the same, "God will save me." A second helicopter flies above, but still his answer is the same, "God will save me." Later that day, as the water level has risen to its highest, he is swept away by the current and is drowned. He ascends to God's presence, angry and disillusioned. He asks God, "Why didn't you help me when I needed you?" God looks at him with love and compassion and answers, "I sent a boat and two helicopters, my son."

The point of this story is that if we ask for help, we will receive it, but whatever way it comes, we must recognize it and take that chance.

Try out different concepts

If they don't make sense or resonate with you, then don't blindly accept them as your own truths—discard them. We all have enough emotional baggage and outdated values to carry without taking on board other people's beliefs, unless they replace our own worn-out ones.

A wise spiritual teacher once said that company is stronger than willpower, so it's important to have met and listened to a person who is going to help facilitate a healing process in our life. We would not go to a surgeon unless he was trained and his success rate was good, so it's unwise to open ourselves up to accept anything less from any practitioner, mentor, or workshop leader.

Taking responsibility for our own health and happiness

We're encouraged to hand the responsibility for our own health to the general practitioner or hospital doctor. In my work as a nurse. I was amazed at the amount of people who took medication because the doctors had prescribed it and didn't know what the long-term effects were. The responsibility for our own health lies with us as individuals.

As a Reiki practitioner, homeopath, and breath work practitioner, my job is to help facilitate someone's healing process.

'I' can heal no one but myself. So there is no such thing as a healer; it's a misleading statement to make about oneself. To take responsibility for one's own health and happiness is a liberating and empowering stance. It gives each of us a chance to make choices for ourselves and to exercise free will.

It's important to remember when approaching the journey of self-healing that we must *want* to take it. Each of us must approach the process for ourselves and ourselves alone. Otherwise, there is no point. We must truly commit.

The searching process

There is a search for that certain 'something' that will help to make sense of all those questions that bounce around inside our minds. It starts with us reading, looking, and experiencing new ideas, books, and situations. It's in that search that we start to go through a process of stages.

Stage one: listening to the talk

At first we may hear a conversation or be in a conversation at a bus stop or dinner party where someone is talking about the questions that have been bouncing around their minds. We may listen and agree, or it may start us thinking again and the search begins in earnest.

Stage two: reading the talk

These conversations may start us reading books, looking for some answers to the questions our minds are posing, which could confirm or refute what we have heard. Or a friend may give us a book which quite literally blows are minds.

Stage three: talking the talk

As we feel more informed, we may start to talk about what we've read with like-minded friends discussing concepts and philosophies.

Stage four: talking the walk

During these discussions, we may go on to talk about meditations, visualizations, affirmations, the power of positive thinking, the law of abundance, spiritual techniques, alternative therapies, the benefits they have, and how they have helped Aunty Gertie with her rheumatism.

Stage five: walking the talk

We may then decide to try out some of these approaches either by attending workshops or practising the techniques described in the books we've been reading.

During the process that I experienced when I committed to self-healing, I realized that we could not address the physical, mental, and emotional dis-ease, disharmony, or needs without being aware and embracing the spiritual.

Committing to a spiritual life

Deepening my commitment to a spiritual life, it became clear to me that this very striving in itself has a tendency to increase the problems at first. Where there is a tendency to be judgmental, we become more judgmental of ourselves. If we have a poor sense of self-worth or indeed self-hatred, it becomes magnified for a while by the very nature of the healing that takes place as we commit to a spiritual life.

So to open deeply, a spiritual life requires that we take tremendous courage and strength, a kind of *warrior spirit*. The strength of the warrior is not in the arm, but in the heart.

And so the process continues…

Stage six: walking the walk

A warrior's heart helps us face our lives more directly, our pains, fears, and limitations, our joys, dreams, and possibilities. This courage allows us to include all aspects of life into our spiritual practice, which brings an integration. With this integration, we contact the divine teacher within (intuition) and we start to progress on our own path.

Stage seven: walking our walk

Each part of this journey is necessary and indeed priceless as it helps us re-define our belief structures, values, boundaries, and goals, but real progress is made while walking our walk. We then move into a totally different way of being; we ascend ourselves and find our unique divinity.

Stage eight: walking the divine's walk

We may then decide to make the final change by aligning our will with the divine's in a life of service and joy.

Reconnecting the neglected soul

It may take years or even lifetimes for a person to arrive at the point where they are walking the divine's walk. It takes courage, absolute discipline, and a deep, deep yearning to get back to love and resolve to keep at the task. Ultimately, it is the reason why we are here—to complete our own self-healing process and free the soul.

The soul is the indestructible part of ourselves, the part that carries on after death, it cannot be hurt or harmed and in essence is perfect, however most of us have lost connection with it and cannot remember its nature and in our forgetfulness have become lost in ego and body identification.

Training the ego

We need to reconnect to our neglected soul so we can care and nurture it. An important part of the journey is training and educating the ego so it will serve the soul instead of it thinking it is the master. When ego thinks it's 'in charge' it can cause chaos and great suffering in our life.

An un-trained ego is much like a puppy, which can be delightful, but hard work. It needs constant correction and training so it will be house trained, walk to heel, know how to behave off the lead, and come back when it is called. With this training, the puppy becomes more delightful and a pleasure to be around. If not trained, it can become a danger to itself and others. It's the same with ego. If that puppy is taken when trained and sent to more training, it can become a guide dog. These dogs are welcomed in places no other dog is allowed. Into shops, restaurants, the theatre, and on flights, to mention a few. In being in service to its master, it changes its very nature from a D.O.G into a G.O.D. When an ego is well trained, it puts itself in service to its master, the soul. If it is not trained, ego will obscure the soul, which leads to neglect because we cannot see it or understand its nature. A lack or loss of connection then ensues.

In other words, training the ego will lead to a healthy connection between our personality, ego, and soul and we will know the totality of self.

My own self-healing process

Two decades ago, while standing at the end of a bed in an intensive care unit, I was facilitating an emergency situation. I was watching a patient go through the most horrific scenario, knowing that the toxicity of the drugs we were administering were killing him faster than the condition he had been admitted for. In that moment, I thought, *"There has to be a better way than this."* Since then, I have been on a quest to find a better way, and that quest has involved heaps of research into a plethora of areas, mainly into energy and energetics.

I commenced my own self-healing, which has included finding a spiritual path with the Self-Realization Fellowship. I practise Kriya Yoga daily and ultimately this has helped me to understand that the best way to nourish myself is to nourish others. Part of my role is to serve others—and that is why I describe myself as a divine waitress.

The power of Breath₄Life™ Breath Work

I believe that we all have a unique divinity within us that we have simply forgotten. That our task in life is to remember all parts of self and become self-realized, it is a journey we all take back to the divine.

The most effective tool I have found in my transformational journey of self-healing is breath work.

We tend to take breathing for granted. It's a fully automatic process. We start to breathe soon after birth and continue without too much interruption until death. What's amazing is it's a fully unconscious process. There is no need to attend consciously to the way we are breathing and we adequately breathe if awake or asleep. It's the same with our heart; it also beats continuously without any conscious effort. We successfully digest food without actually having to do anything about it too. There are thousands of vital processes occurring in our bodies on a daily basis, of which we are unaware and uninformed. It just all happens and this part of the workings of the body is driven by unconscious intelligence, which frees up our conscious awareness for other pursuits.

What is exciting about the breath is that it can be completely unconscious, but it can also become a conscious, intentional practice. It's a unique quality and makes it a link between the conscious and unconscious aspects of our being.

If you want to you can decide to stop breathing for a couple of minutes. Then you can resume at any time you like. You can fill your lungs completely with breath, or breathe very lightly, or let the air out in a gentle sigh, or blow it out with force, all because you want to. It is within your conscious control. So it is a simple matter to bring consciousness to the act of breathing.

Conscious breathing

There are many different 'teachings of the breath' that teach us how to bring consciousness to the act of breathing. These have shown us that it is of great physical, mental, emotional, and spiritual benefit to the human individual. Most Eastern traditions and Karl Jung state that 'the quickest way to change your consciousness is to change the way you are breathing.'

Conscious breathing encourages the expansion of consciousness. To inhale consciously is to positively excite and expand our whole environment. To exhale consciously is to support the relaxation of our surroundings and connecting energies. Every moment of conscious breath is an inspired co-creation with the whole of life itself.

When I first created the Breath$_4$Life™ Breath Work program, I brought the knowledge and experience of my own self-healing. I produced an exciting, dynamic, unique, cutting-edge self-healing process, which deals with all levels of self, all levels of consciousness, and all levels of energy. Healing occurs on a physical, mental, emotional, and spiritual level. It is more than conscious connected breath work as it uses specific techniques to go deeper into the subconscious. It clears patterns of old limiting beliefs, destructive patterns of behavior, and heart clutter. It helps us re-align ourselves with that bigger part of ourselves. It is a life-transforming journey of self-discovery into self-awareness and freedom.

Releasing suppressed emotions with breath work

If you have suppressions of guilt or anger, which are so widespread in our society today, you may experience frequent outbursts, upset, frustration, and even physical disease. You may find yourself taking that anger out on someone you love, like your friend, lover, or child, when what you really want to experience with that person is love and joy. A typical reaction when something like that happens is to wonder, "What came over me?" not realizing that you have tapped into a suppressed emotion, which controls your behavior.

Breath work can help release any of these 'heavier emotions' in a safe environment, leaving you feeling both grounded, calmer, and more alive.

It is easy to confuse these heavier emotions as negative ones, yet in reality no emotion is 'negative'; it is just our perception that tells us it is so. An emotion is 'energy in motion' ranging from the subtle to the intense, from apathetic to enraged, or from being content to absolute bliss.

Categorizing them as 'bad' or 'good' misses the point of our emotions entirely. It is far more constructive to see emotions as messengers, assisting us through life's journey. When we wander a little too far off the path, so called 'bad emotions' warn us of our detour, and nudge us in the right direction again. This often is felt in our solar plexus area, butterflies in the stomach, or just a sense of general unease. These gut feelings are powerful indicators of where our thoughts and feelings are taking us, and acknowledging them, whether they are indeed 'good' or 'bad,' is a healthy process.

It's important to actually process all states of emotion. Instead of resisting them, welcome them in, which helps re-integrate the energy into our energy field, rather than being stuck in the body. This fluidity enhances the body's natural bio-feedback, encouraging health and well-being.

In conclusion

Everybody can learn to breathe well—it's just a matter of being more present to the process of breathing itself. If a stressful situation arises, it's important to keep the breath moving, which helps to reduce suppressions within the body.

Breath4Life™ Breath Work has helped hundreds of people re-gain a true sense of self and liberated them from past traumas, limiting beliefs, and unhelpful behavioral patterns.

***

To Contact Pennie:

http://www.acorntooak.org.uk/pages/about-breathwork

Richard A. Oden

Rockdale County Commission Chairman & CEO Richard A. Oden took office January 2009. Voters re-elected him to a second term in 2012.

Under his administration, Rockdale has earned five consecutive awards for excellence in financial management reporting and maintained an AA2 and AA3 bond rating the past six years. He also:

- Represents Georgia on the National Association of Counties' National Board of Directors;
- Chaired several Atlanta Regional Commission committees, leading the charge on issues including transportation, economic development, water, energy, housing, and natural resources;
- Graduated from the Association of County Commissioners of Georgia's Certified Commissioners Advanced Program.
- Recipient of Jack & Jill of America, Inc., East Suburban Atlanta Chapter's 2013 Community Service Award;
- Received the National Association of Minority Contractors' 2011 Trailblazer Award;
- Named among Atlanta Business League's 2009 Men of Influence Class.

A graduate of Kent State University, Mr. Oden is a lifetime member of the Golden Flash Club and served as Captain of KSU's 1972 Mid-American Conference Championship Football Team, where his coaches and teammates voted him Most Inspirational Player.

The Change[9]

Mr. Oden and his wife Josett have been married for 32 years. Together they have five children and seven grandchildren.

Uncovering Your Greatness

By Richard A. Oden

When I first received an email from Jim Britt and Jim Lutes on July 21, 2015 and they revealed they were bringing new people to the forefront in the intra-industry of personal development, I instantly knew I was going to step forward, invest my time and resources, and become a co-author and partner in the Change Book Series Project.

For more than five (5) decades, I have been sharpening my craft in the personal development and improvement profession. I have experienced maybe more temporary failures than most people I know and probably more people whom I don't know.

I am briefly going to share with you, from personal experiences in this chapter, my 60-plus years of dealing with and living with stumbling-blocks, setbacks, tragedies, disappointments, heartbreaks, and all kinds of adverse discouragers that would eliminate or kill most people then I am going to show you from my proven track record and experiences just how to overcome these negative bothers of doom and then how to turn your world around while moving you towards peak performance and greatness.

Fronting and Overcoming Adversity

In life, every one of us will always experience difficult and challenging times throughout our lifetime. None of us are exempt from living and dealing with troubled waters; this is a fact of life. Here are a few (and I mean a few) of my own personal life experiences that I have been able to draw strength and hope from that have launch me forward toward my recognition of personal development and improvement.

The Change[9]

Setbacks: After a knee injury, and winning a Division I college football conference championship and participating in a major national college bowl game, I was not drafted into the NFL. This action literally broke my heart at the age of 22, which grabbed a large chunk of my spirit from me.

My attitude became so adverse that I ended up in a deep tailspin towards self-destruction. Shortly after moving to Atlanta with all the setbacks, I became homeless, which was very painful, demoralizing, and demeaning; I was in the dumps!

Heartbreaks: After the football setback, my older brother overdosed on drugs while living in Los Angeles, CA. He didn't have any money or insurance. Our family had to handle his final arrangements. He had an attitude of hustle, the behavior of a so-call player, and other metaphors.

After the loss of my brother, another family heartbreak occurred. My nine-year-old niece passed away from cancer; the next year my mother's brother and sister passed away; then my father passed away that same year.

Tragedy: Many years later while working for a major corporation, I became a victim and survivor of multiple gunshot wounds in a botched robbery attempt on my life.

I was shot three (3) times in one incident—one bullet entered inches below my heart, which caused life-threatening injuries to my stomach, bowel/intestines, and liver; another bullet entered my left bicep and exited my triceps; and the final bullet entered into my left thigh and exited through my buttock.

These life-changing experiences and my near-death tragedy episode demonstrated to me how critical and important the power of thought and what and how you think really plays a significant role in all of our lives. Therefore, in this account of "Uncovering Your Greatness" (UYG), I am going to share a few strategies that will launch you onto a higher level of abundant living while showing you how to live in greatness.

Your Perception and Attitude is Your Starting Point to Greatness!

Your mind is a terrible thing to waste… It's all about your thoughts and your thinking! The book of Genesis tells us… *You have authority, favor and dominion over every living thing that moveth upon earth.* This also specifically includes your thinking… This is where your greatness is born!

Greatness starts with your perception and attitude; when you gain a better understanding of how your thoughts affect you and your quality of life; when you learn how your perception of yourself is the starting point to your self-discovery; when you learn how your perception of yourself and your environment determines your attitude, then you'll realize how significant a role the Universal Invisible Law of Cause and Effect plays in the awareness of yourself and in your thinking.

I have learned through experience that one's perception (self-awareness) and attitude will help you or hurt you! In fact you can develop a positive mental attitude and achieve all your goals and desires but still not have a good perception of yourself. That means it is possible to have low self-esteem and low self-awareness with a positive mental attitude and not be happy with your life. If that is the case, then you'll experience a false sense of happiness.

With a positive consciousness, you can teach and train yourself to remain positive in most and all situations. Even when things take a drastic turn for the worst, it is possible for you to remain positive by blocking out negativity and quickly focusing on the positive or objective aspects of the situation.

It doesn't matter what the negativity may be—you'll teach and train yourself to remain optimistic. In our profession, we see this every day: a person who has achieved material success, who has climbed

The Change

the ladder of accomplishment, or a person who has collected huge amounts of money and wealth, but still lives a life of misery, unhappiness, and sorrow.

The main reason is because they have overlooked the first step in self-discovery. Regardless of who you are or where you now stand, it's never too late to uncover your true feelings or uncover the real perception (self-awareness) of who you really are!

From my proven lifelong experiences, trials, and tribulations, I am able to show you strategies on how to search deep inside yourself to uncover your true self! I will be able to show you how to build an even more powerful and emotional you to deal with the emotions of others.

I have learned from experience that having a clear and concise perception of who you are allows you to develop an attitude about yourself whether it's positive or negative.

This is where you will need to make a choice, which road are you going to travel in life?

The Power of Knowing Who You Are!

You are a spiritual, mental, emotional, and physical being! Your mental element is centered on an attitude—and an attitude is an organization of motives around an individual's response to a person, situation, or institution. An attitude of acceptance and rejection may be called "love and "hate."

Such attitudes are not simple emotions or motives because they cannot exist apart from a relationship to a person or object, and because of the situation they may call forth different emotions at different times, and still be consistent with the core of the attitude.

The Side Kick to Attitude is Self-Concept

Your Self-Concept is to remember while you are developing your attitudes toward life, remember that your attitudes also relate to the situation in your environment. Every attitude involves a relationship between two major elements: the environmental situation or element to which it is directed and the effects of that element or situation upon you as a person.

Think about it, your attitude involves not the situation alone or the person alone, but it involves both, the relationship between the two—the person and the situation.

What you think and how you think is a learned anticipation that you will accept or be accepted in certain circumstance or that you will reject or be rejected. This attitudinal behavior can be called the self-concept!

Your self-concept is a pattern of attitudes and is learned in the same way as other attitudes. It is said that there is nothing basic or intrinsic about your self-concept. You are not born with it; it's the integration of countless learning experiences. Like other attitudes, the self-concept has an influence on discernment and enthusiasm in new situations.

Did you know that your self-concept (self-attitude, self-image) shapes new experiences to conform to its already established pattern? Your behavior can be understood as you attempt to maintain the consistency of your self-concept.

Understanding the Harmonious Properties and Impacts to Greatness

YOUR MIND! How your mind actually works to attract your goals, objectives, your dreams and desires!

Your <u>conscious</u> is defined as knowing, aware, having feeling, or knowledge (of one's own sensations, feelings etc., or external things): knowing or feeling (that something is, was happening or existing); cognizant.

Your <u>subconscious</u> is occurring without conscious perception, or with only slight perception on the part of the individual; said of mental processes and reactions; not fully conscious; imperfectly aware—the subconscious mental activity: term now rarely used in psychiatry.

The <u>mind</u> is to think, whence spirit, force, memory, recollection, or remembrance; what one thinks; opinion, that which thinks, perceives, feels, wills, etc., seat or subject of consciousness. The conscious and subconscious together as a unit; psyche [the reactionary mind].

These definitions clearly explain and show us all that we can control the way we think and therefore we can control our destiny. We can control the way we choose to live and where to live, where we work, and whom we work for. It very clear that the choice is ours as individuals! It's your choice!

The Impact and Power of Your Thoughts

Once you realize that how you react to life is a result of your thoughts processes and accept responsibility for your actions, only then can you move forward. If you are willing to travel with me and pay attention to the powers of your thoughts, then I will show and share with you how to attract the goodness from life and how to walk in your purpose.

There is a formula for achieving personal excellence and greatness… I can show you how to get there.

Developing a Crystal Clear Image

Habits, attitudes, and one's purpose are all forms of learned behaviors and also function as springboards of human action.

When you have a clearly defined picture of who you are, you will release such a powerful burst of energy into the atmosphere; which will result in the universal law of cause and effect in sending back to you the capacity to transform your thoughts into action; or better yet bring your dreams closer to reality. I can and will be able to show you more on this topic when we get together soon.

Nature's Universal Invisible Law of Cause and Effect

Nature's Universal Invisible Law of Cause and Effect is an invisible boomerang, what is sometimes known as what goes around, comes around. It's the do unto others as you would have them do unto you. It's seek and ye shall find belief, it's the knock on the door and it shall be open, to the hidden pathway and silent principles and practices of life.

When you begin to see your challenges, obstacles, disappointments, stumbling-blocks, setbacks, negativity, and temporary failures as stepping stones, bridge builders, and learning blocks, then your world will start moving forward through personal power development and process performance improvement experiences.

The Universal Invisible Law of Cause and Effect works every time, all the time, it cannot see or hear; it does not discriminate; it doesn't care whether you are rich or poor, old or young, big or small. This invisible quality of life enhancer is guaranteed to all who identify its powers and utilize it!

The Universal Invisible Law of Cause and Effect is a gift from above that just silently goes about its business of getting actual results for the sender! This is one of the pathways where you can tap into your greatness!

This hidden never-ending powerful tool is found in Nature's Great Universal Invisible Law of Cause and Effect. I can show you how to use it to help you increase your personal power, professional excellence in performance while improving your processes!

Greatness Can Become Realty!

In "Uncovering Your Greatness" (UYG) approach, the utilization of human resource which includes know-how, experience, knowledge, skills, talent, and abilities teamed up with the proper attitude, behavior, discipline, habits, and applied action will result in increased performance, productivity, effectiveness, and efficiency.

The continued success in any situation will largely depend on the development of an optimistic consciousness, a clearly defined purpose, teamed up with discipline and a burning personal and team desire to achieve greatness.

In any situation, achieving excellence or greatness entirely depends upon the strength of the human capital in your environment or organization. When a leader in the organization is able show his team how to unleash their full potential, then the team or organization will position itself for accomplishing excellence or greatness.

The establishment of individual and team discipline is paramount. By holding everyone on the team or in the organization accountable will result in improved and increased effectiveness and efficiency; while at the same time releasing into the atmosphere a powerful magnetic energy that will attract the desired planned result.

When you learn how to utilize the Uncovering Your Greatness (UYG) approach, you will be able to bring into your world a powerful magnetic energy and tool that will achieve results. UYG will achieve strategic and tactical results by holding people, teams, and your organization accountable.

Having a clearly defined purpose which serves as your guide will align the team and organization's plan and efforts towards the attainment of the goals and objectives that were planned.

Herein is a tangible real time activity of how the powers of the mind (maintaining a positive consciousness) can and will work when applied with unquestioned faith, belief, and courage, followed by having clearly defined specific goals and objectives teamed up with results-oriented action plans for achievement.

Achieving Greatness through Team

In 2014, utilizing the Uncovering Your Greatness (UYG) approach, the Rockdale County Government Directors and Leadership teams started working through the newly created and introduced Rockdale County Government Operating Efficiency System called the R-GOES™.

R-GOES™ was designed to break down silos and internal barriers to communication to bring team members closer together, address conflict head on with strategies to tackle issues, resolve conflicts as a team while forging forward with an even more harmonious team work environment.

Because of this UYG approach, namely strategic and innovative outlook on developing creative ways to resolve conflicts and issues, the organization is moving toward creating a peak performance high-energy team work environment.

This organization and team members, as a unit, came up with workable solutions as a team on how to improve and increase organizational effectiveness, productivity, and efficiency; which will put the organization in a better position to become a more customer service-oriented organization; internal and external.

The R-GOES™ TEAM of directors and leadership bought into the UYG approach of exceeding customer's expectation with a clearly defined purpose.

The UYG approach can show you and your organization how to accomplish similar results, while at the same time improving your personal and professional development.

The Value and Power of Connecting the DOTs

When a person or team learn how to use the power of developing and maintaining positive consciousness and then tie this attitude, behavior, habit, and practice to the powerful universal invisible law of cause and effect, your world will literally and figuratively change forever.

UYG can show you the proven steps on how to tap into this amazing quality of life personal and professional enhancer that will change your life. This tried and tested strategy and approach has a proven track record of getting favorable results.

Where do you want to be in the future? How do you plan on getting there? No matter where you now stand, you can literally impact change in your life today! When you are able or learn how to connect the dots more times than not, then you will be walking in your destiny or what I call uncovering your greatness. UYG can show you how to get the results you are looking for in the now!

Richard's added value offer to living a rewarding and balanced life

The Power and Value of Volunteerism through Civic and Community Engagement

UYG approach also encourages giving back. Success is an ongoing give and receive process. Herein, are other measurable results-oriented processes and performance improvement activities by connecting the power of positive consciousness to civic engagement where your input, energies, and strategies can assist others to improve their agency/organization performance and productivity.

Volunteering and giving of oneself in service without pay is an invaluable lifetime and transformation experience. In fact, this attitude, behavior, and habit has allowed me to gain a wide array of proven results, leadership skills, knowledge, policy making, talent expansion in management, brand and marketing, community relations, customer service, sales, executive and life coaching; along with developing personal and proficient enhancement experiences and know-how in successfully leading teams while accomplishing favorable processes and performance improvement results.

This chapter in the *Change Book Series # 8* with Jim Britt and Jim Lutes, along with the other co-authors, is a great resource tool for anyone from any walk of life to tap into the variety of unique stories and experiences of other successful professionals in the intra-personal development industry. My chapter on Uncovering Your Greatness (UYG) is only a snapshot of what my 50-plus years of personal and professional growth and development, relationship building and experiences have allowed me to share with you.

"The stars are at your fingertips, and the world has always been yours, so reach out for your better world today because the world awaits the missing YOU!"

***

To Contact Richard:

Alexander At'Ta Associates, Inc.

Conyers, Georgia 30012.

Telephone: 770-860-8442

Email: raoden@alexander-atta.com

Website: www.alexander-atta.com

Shelby Molchan

Shelby Molchan is considered by many to be Northern Nevada's foremost Colon Hydrotherapist specializing in degenerative disease detoxification.

Shelby began her medical career at the age of 18 starting out as a receptionist for a prominent OB/GYN in Burbank, CA. Focusing on patient social skills, she became office manager and upon the doctor's retirement, began a home-based medical billing service.

She also attended beauty school and spent a number of years as a stay home mom until, following a lengthy illness, at the age of 42 she became a Certified Colon Hydrotherapist. Shelby worked at alternative medical clinics in Reno and Carson City, and numerous doctors in the area referred their degenerative disease patients to her for Colon Hydrotherapy treatments that include coffee, ozone, and probiotic implants. During and since her illness, she studied the emotional, spiritual, and lifestyle aspects of detoxification and healing to build a wealth of information that she shared through her writings for a local health publication. Shelby coaches clients on cleansing, nutrition, and lifestyle changes, believes in educating people to understand their body's needs, and is honored to be a part of *The Change* book series!

Would You Change To Save Your Life?

By Shelby Molchan

Changing your personal world to save your life is a monumental undertaking. Healing a sick body requires a commitment to self-discovery, a commitment to learning, and a commitment to change.

The body is mechanically designed to repair itself in many situations. It is also designed to manifest symptoms when assistance is needed from the outside. The immune system is your body's amazing protector and self-healer and seventy percent of it resides in the gut. During times of illness, boosting the immune system gives your body what it needs to fight back. As the vehicle of your spirit, your body requires respect, care, and attention to its distress signals. Recognizing the body's signals is of great benefit in the role of self-healing. Becoming in touch with the body includes acting on intuition, which allows you to begin to understand signals for assistance and helps you to be proactive in self-care. Acting on your intuition brings insights and ideas on how to bring about changes necessary for healing.

At the age of 42, I changed my life in order to regain my health. Suffering from postpartum hemorrhage, anemia, and exhaustion, I spent the better part of a year lying in bed bleeding. I had been blessed with a strong body and sharp mind my entire life, until I found myself dopey and weak, unable to get out of bed without nearly passing out. It was a humbling experience. I have always been a 'high-energy' girl and I had a lot on my plate at that time. There was no time for me to be bedridden, even for a week, yet my illness lasted nearly a year. My newborn and three year old were left in the care of my husband and teenage daughter. I felt like a burden to them and fought depression along with my illness. I mean, what can you do when you're too sick to get out of bed, but lie there and think about how bad things are, right?

Wrong! I was aware enough at the time to understand that negative thinking could block my ability to heal. I opened my window so I could see the beauty of nature and gave thanks for it every day. The experience of my illness began a healing journey for me using prayer, meditation, visualization, and daydreaming. My body was imprisoned by illness, but my spirit was free. I visualized myself healthy and free of bleeding. I imagined myself running and playing with my kids. I daydreamed about swimming in the ocean, hiking, and planting my garden. Every day I prayed for the strength to cook dinner or help with the kids. I held crystal rocks, used essential oils, and stuck acupuncture needles in trigger points associated with the uterus, bleeding, and anemia. Eventually, the bleeding subsided and I was able to resume some daily duties.

During my healing journey, I researched alternative and natural methods of self-healing. Colon Hydrotherapy had come up more than once. But at that time in my life, I was not in the habit of listening to my intuition. My ego said that my uterus was the cause, not my colon, so I ignored prompts to cleanse. As my strength returned, I became more in touch with my body's signals. I began to question mental messages that did not seem to feel right. Disregarding the ego's messages is not easy, since the ego is designed to be our protector. The ego was designed to instigate such things as our 'fight or flight' reaction and as humankind has evolved, we no longer constantly require such drastic measures on the physical plane. We now require connection to subtle signals the body sends prior to the onset of illness to keep us safe from hidden dangers in our environment. We need to tap into our intuition to protect us from threats such as overexposure to electromagnetic frequencies, contaminated food, or toxic environments.

For me, messages about cleansing grew stronger and louder, until I could not ignore the signals any longer. I gave Colon Hydrotherapy a try, and after experiencing a number of treatments and seeing how they enhanced my well-being, I became motivated to try some of the diet and lifestyle changes my therapist had been recommending. I started with changes that intuitively felt good and were the easiest for me to incorporate into my life. Positive, lasting change often occurs in baby steps.

When the opportunity to become trained as a Colon Hydrotherapist came, I knew it was what I wanted. I was already a believer and now it would be my chance to help others reclaim their health, as I had been able to. I knew going in that healing the body, mine and others, was more than just cleansing the colon. True healing occurs when a person embraces the idea of change, whether it means committing to eating all organic food or removing oneself from unhealthy situations. Healing occurs by a change in vibrational frequency. Taking spiritual steps, such as prayer and meditation, can return the body, mind, and spirit to a peaceful, loving vibration. With realignment to the higher source (the divine spirit within) healing then occurs on many levels.

Lifestyle changes required for healing and staying healthy range from simple tweaking to radical changes affecting diet, exercise, relationships, prolonged stress, environmental toxicity, and conscious thought process. Chronic fear, anger, and prolonged stress weaken the immune system. Immunity repair is crucial to degenerative disease patients, especially those who have undergone modern medicine's immunity depleting treatments and medications. Properly feeding the body, while reducing the intake of toxins, is crucial to healing as this allows overworked body systems and organs to catch up.

A toxic liver is one of the main issues related to degenerative disease today. Colon Hydrotherapy and coffee enemas detoxify the liver, which retains residuals of many pharmaceuticals, heavy metals, and parasites. Cleansing the liver assists the body in purging physical toxins as well as negative emotional energy. Relieving the liver of its toxic overload helps change the individual's perception from one of negativity and anger to hope and possibility. Traditional Chinese Medicine recognizes that emotional Chi resides in the liver and that the kidneys house fear. Anger and fear compromise healing. Removing oneself from hostile environments and reducing exposure to negative media are major factors in recalibrating the body.

People are naturally resistant to giving up their constant connection to media, including much of the negativity it portrays. Conscious monitoring, to reduce daily exposure to negativity and drama, has a profound effect on healing. There is a lot to deal with out there. Environmental and electromagnetic pollutants are at an all-time high. Our materialistic lifestyles propel us to always want more and the amount of chemicals in our food alone is enough to make people sick.

Cleansing is essential to remove accumulated toxins the body has stored over its lifetime. Most people don't just get sick overnight. Usually it's a slow downward slide that is acknowledged as aging, just slowing down, or not feeling as good as we used to. Media and the medical establishment confirms the programming that as we age, we should expect to slow down and begin to manifest a list of ailments. Conveniently, there is a list of pharmaceuticals designed to treat the symptoms of aging. But actually, it is very realistic to be pharmaceutical free in your fifties and beyond! This slow decline is actually the body becoming bogged down by toxins to the point that the filtering systems of the body become overwhelmed and autointoxication sets in, greatly accelerating the aging process. Sadly, the aging process has descended to the teenage and young twenties group. More and younger people are suffering from symptoms and taking medications than ever before. Treating symptoms with medications often masks underlying issues that when addressed with nutrition and cleansing can eliminate both the symptoms and the medications.

Many people believe cleansing is not necessary, and for the healthy individual, maybe not. It is of interest to note that over 2000 years ago, before chemical fertilizer and pesticides, electromagnetic fields and pollution, Jesus found it prudent to fast to cleanse the body. Buddha said that it was necessary to cleanse the body in order to keep the mind clear and sound. That was more than a thousand years before Christ. These references and my personal experiences and observations confirm to me that cleansing is of benefit to everyone!

I have worked as a Colon Hydrotherapist in several alternative clinics, primarily treating degenerative disease patients. I have seen patients with health challenges ranging from simple to complex, to life threatening. They come surrounded by family and friends for support, while others come alone. They all come with a commitment to take healing into their own hands. Those with an "I'm not ready to die!" attitude propel themselves towards self-healing miracles. Denying a death prediction with positive action is an important step. After all, how many times has the prognosis been wrong? Who but God knows how much time a person has left to live on this earth?

I have witnessed 'hopeless' cases recover and become strong, healthy individuals with bright futures. Their positive results evolved from their own efforts and the loving support of caretakers, including family, friends, and the caregiving professionals that serve them. In contrast, I have treated people who should recover quickly, only to linger and decline. Mental attitude has everything to do with it. Caretakers that do not support the patient's intuitive need for change hold the patient back. Negative influences or fear-based caretakers hamper the patient's ability to intuitively implement needed healing therapies. I encourage my clients to take stock of their entire life with an intention to recognize the changes that are necessary. Since you don't know what you don't know, recognizing and accepting insights for change can be a large part of the battle. Refusal to make necessary life changes limits the ability to completely recover from a serious health challenge.

Food can either heal or slowly break down the immune system. We do what is quick and easy—especially when we feel poorly. That leads to choices that are not always healthy ones. For example, look around the supermarket at the grocery carts filled with prepackaged foods and sodas, then look at the drivers of those carts. In most cases, they tend not to be the picture of health and happiness. Eating a diet of processed, chemically enhanced food does not provide long-term energy or appropriate nutrition. It has saddened me to observe cancer patients in the IV rooms of alternative clinics eating out of fast food bags. When the body is fighting for life, it requires nutrient-dense food to provide the extra energy required for the healing process. Indeed, nutrition is something most people have received incorrect programming about. Common belief is, that there are enough standards and regulations with regard to food production that there would not be anything 'bad' for you in the grocery store.

The truth is that about 80% of food today is genetically modified. Non-organic food may not only be genetically modified, but tainted with fertilizers, pesticides, artificial colors and flavors, all of which are foreign to the body. These chemicals create extra strain on the liver, which is the body's major filter for these types of things.

There is no cookie cutter for health. People often ask me what I do for myself, wanting to just copy my methods. If it were that easy we would all be healthy! I am continually learning how to care for and live comfortably in my body. And I want you to know that after years of learning what works for me, now in my fifties, I have more energy, less pain, and I am much more content in my life than ever before. Getting to personally know 'you' is the secret!

Sometimes clients are too weak and overwhelmed from procedures, medications, lack of support, and pain to take on large lifestyle

The Change[9]

changes. When this is the case, I encourage them to begin with positive visualization. Visualization is something that the sickest, weakest person can do all day long, simply by directing thoughts in a consciously positive manner. Using the Law of Attraction to fight illness on a mental level is one of the most effective tools a sick person has. Everything we think, say, and do sends vibrational frequencies into the universe that attract like frequencies. This means, positive energy attracts positive energy and negative energy attracts negative energy. You may be thinking that it would be too difficult to monitor all thoughts, words, and actions. Initially it seems like a lot, but just by being conscious of what thoughts you are having brings about a change. Back to 'you don't know what you don't know,' meaning as soon as you recognize that a thought is not in line with what you are trying to manifest, you can strike that thought and replace it with a new positive thought.

Your body uses neurological pathways to communicate with the brain. Having the same thoughts and doing the same actions create patterns. We like to repeat the same patterns because our ego-mind has determined that a certain way of thinking or doing is comfortable and safe. This is where many people get stuck. Even when desiring change, you may find yourself repeating habits because they are easy, comfortable, and you don't know any other way. This is living by default. Once you recognize this, the door to change has been opened. Consciously making new decisions that are in the best interest of self forges new behavioral pathways to the brain. Continuing to recognize negative patterns and make adjustments helps the conscious self to make better choices. At first, this can be difficult to enact because it takes you out of your comfort zone. So, I refer you back to cleansing, meditation, and prayer since they lift vibrational frequency, which creates new options.

Daily meditation puts us in touch with our hearts. With continued practice, we soon begin to wonder about the value of some of our repetitive life habits that no longer bring joy or inspire us.

Meditation itself is a difficult concept for people to justify within the busy demands of everyday life. So we say now is not a good time, but now IS the perfect time, before illness affects our life. The human body needs a break from stress and distractions and meditation provides that relief. While the mind has unlimited ability and potential, the human body has many limits.

Addressing the heart's desires for life can be of great benefit to achieving good health. Many people in the world today are leaving unfulfilling or toxic situations to pursue their calling. Listening to the heart leads to positive, life-altering change. Following the heart brings joy as well as renewed energy to a depressed and stagnant body. It is frightful to acknowledge the fact that you may need to leave your job or spouse because staying is not promoting your higher good. The ego brings forth all kinds of scary scenarios about what could happen following that type of change. This alone keeps many paralyzed by fear. But, if the ego is quieted and we ask ourselves what good can come of it, we often get a long list of positive outcomes that when examined are aligned with the heart. Focusing on that list brings solutions previously believed to be impossible.

Society tells us to go to school, then college, build credit, buy a car, buy a house, etc. So we do it every day, over and over, just to pay those bills. Before we know it, we have made choices that make us feel shackled to debt, a stressful job, or unhealthy situations. Michael Bernard Beckwith said, "Out of nothing and no way, a way will be made." That quote plays constantly in my mind when I'm feeling challenged.

I have witnessed people do the personal work necessary to heal. However, once healed, they returned to the lifestyle that made them ill in the first place. They failed to embrace an ongoing personal commitment to continuing healthy lifestyle adjustments in order to maintain their new level of health. The immortal ego may convince you that you can get away with this, but only doing enough work to achieve the desired outcome does not provide lasting change; it only creates the seesaw effect. Because of the way the Law of Attraction works, the moment you revert back to old habits, the universe begins to prepare to send back the old results. Who wants that?

When someone says they cannot seem to change their life, it is because the individual does now know how, believes it's too hard, or simply fears it. Clients have told me they are too old or it is too late for them, but the bottom line is, age is not a factor and it's never too late when the heart's desire is better health, comfort, and peace. Changing your life is like yoga; you can always improve upon the process, meaning it is a practice.

I encourage you to practice visualizing the change you would like to see in your own life and in the world. Hold that vision in your heart. Daydream about it. Pray, meditate, and keep building the scenario in your mind. Think positively of it and soon you will notice changes appearing. Be observant, the changes may be small at first, but remember, lasting change occurs in baby steps. A lifelong commitment to growth and health, with bold acceptance that everything changes anyway, brings amazing levels of health and joy into your world. Don't delay, begin your change today!

***

To Contact Shelby:

www.ShelbyMolchan.com

Sherry Brantley

Sherry Brantley is the author of *STEPP—Start To Exercise Personal Power—How To Create Positive Change in Your Life!* She is a Certified Life Coach and is a dynamic leader and trainer specializing in the areas of *Goal-Setting and Goal-Getting!*

Sherry's passionate purpose is to assist people in making positive choices in their daily lives, effecting positive change by recognizing and utilizing their Personal Power while respecting and accepting the Personal Power of others.

Using proven techniques developed through both her STEPP and her R.A.V.E. (Recognize, Analyze, Visualize, & Empowerize) programs, participants prepare personalized plans designed to propel them to accomplish their goals.

As a leading parenting instructor for Michigan State University's *Building Strong Families* program, Sherry was successful in teaching parents, teachers, and caregivers how to develop positive communication skills, and assisted them in utilizing techniques that were helpful in achieving the dynamics of a positive family structure. Her book, *Seven Successful Strategies for Divorced Parents,* highlights easy-to-use techniques which families can immediately implement to improve various areas of their personal and interpersonal lives, including communication, health, finances, and more.

Change The Beliefs That Keep You In Grief

By Sherry Brantley

Chances are you've faced some type of fear in your life. Perhaps you were facing fears that were only in your mind and through your vivid imagination, you managed to conjure up the worst-case scenarios for a given event. Or maybe you were faced with an outstanding opportunity that could have proven to be perfect for you, and yet—you allowed your *negative* self-talk to get in the way of ushering in the needed change. Or worse still, *you* may have felt confident with forging ahead on a particular goal, dream, or project, but after consulting with the 'naysayers' and doom-players,' fear took a stronghold and refused to let go.

Yes, we've all had to face our fears at some point. As with anything, we can allow fear to overtake us, limit our life choices, and keep us on a debilitating road in our lives. Or, we can resolve to recognize our fears, analyze them to determine why we hold or create certain beliefs or fears, and vow to release them once and for all.

Metathesiophobia is the fear of change, and while most of us don't have a morbid anxiety surrounding change, this type of fear is very prevalent in the daily lives of many people, to some degree. Fear of having to change jobs, fear of losing a marriage or a relationship with a significant other, fear of a major move across country, fearing you don't truly have what it takes to *really* start your own business, or just a fear of following your passion keeps many people living a mediocre life, just wondering what their lives could be/feel/look like if only they had the courage to move forward.

Another fear that grips many people is Xenophobia—fear of the unfamiliar. I often think of a short story in relation to this fear:

There was once a young soldier that had been captured and taken behind enemy lines. His tormentors allowed him two choices: He could confront the firing squad the next morning, or he could walk through a door which was marked 'Unknown Fears." The young soldier chose the firing squad. After his execution, the leader of his tormentors was asked what was behind the mysterious door. "Freedom," he replied, "but very few people are willing to deal with their fear of the unknown."

Once you clearly understand the freedom that awaits you with releasing your fears, you will be amazed at the type of life you are able to lead!

The universal law of attraction states: What you focus on in your life—you expand in your life, or simply put: *What we constantly think about, we bring about—whether we want it or not.* If you want a clear picture of what the universe will be offering to you, simply reflect on the thoughts and actions which you deliver from within. Do they stem from a platform of love? Of appreciation? Of genuine gratitude? Or are they based on and steeped in or around your fears?

Once focused and committed to your own spiritual growth and unleashing your Personal Power, your inner vision opens and your horizons expand. A truth that needs to be clearly understood is this: *Once you become committed to a thing, be it negative or positive, the laws of the universe automatically align themselves to your commitment in equal proportion.* As powerful as the universal laws are, they cannot remove our very belief system from us—we must do that ourselves. The universal laws work *with* us—never against us. Hence, if we're working in a negative mode, they can only work *with* us to continue those negative patterns. If we are working from a positive place, the positive forces of the universe must align with us. The universe, in working *with* us, actually works *for* us. But it allows us to decide which route to pour those energies into—negative or positive. *That is the only time and way the universe acts in a neutral manner.* Once we've chosen, however, it goes all the way—full force to act on our beliefs, our thought system. Surely, our very thoughts hold the power of the universe within them. You must take a moment to grasp this truth in order to really begin to understand the impact it can truly make in your life.

Allow me to share a realization of the powerful law of attraction working in my own life, knocking out my fears and gently prodding me to move forward with my goals:

My youngest daughter had completed high school and was preparing to embark on a life of her own away from home. While some parents experience the 'empty nest' syndrome, I was anything but that. 'Ecstatic' would be the term I would use for how I felt. Years before, through having been divorced, I began raising my three young daughters solo. My ex-husband was unemployed and therefore, I was a single parent without the benefit of receiving child support, and my girls and I had experienced our share of the 'lean years.'

Now, with my youngest daughter moving onward and upward, I felt I no longer wanted a home to maintain, and dreams of moving to where I'd longed to be, Arizona, swam through my head daily. I decided to downsize and I placed my home on the market. Some naysayers in the form of neighbors stopped by to inform me that my home would not sell quickly and that there was simply no way I'd be able to receive the asking price listed for the home.

Not only did it sell within four weeks, but the buyer did not quibble nor negotiate. She offered to buy at the price it was listed for!

After selling my home and moving into an apartment, my employer downsized and eliminated the department I'd been working in. As a result, I obtained a telemarketing job at a local bank in my area. To say that I was unhappy was an understatement. The sales quotas we had to meet each day became more and more unattainable and the employees had to adhere to a specific amount of minutes when going to the restroom!

I had always believed there was more to my life than I'd created, and with my newfound belief system stating *'we only experience that which we create,'* I pondered: *What is it I truly want to create and therefore experience in my life?* That night, I decided what I truly wanted was to finally move to the state of my destination—Arizona. I'd never even been to Arizona. Granted, the state of Michigan is a beautiful state with its four seasons and vibrant colors of nature. After four and a half decades there, however, I longed to live in an area that had a warmer climate year-round. I realized I could not *change the state of the weather,* but I could *change whether I lived in that state!*

I began to visualize what it would feel like to move to Arizona. Besides being warm, I envisioned me living in a beautiful apartment in an upscale area. I saw friendly neighbors, shopping centers, and lots of things to do. Knowing that fear feeds off of inaction, I made my decision to move on a Saturday evening and took action to post my resume online that very night.

I even took the liberty to call my daughters and my closest friends to tell them I was moving. For years, they'd heard me talk of moving to Arizona and after the initial shock of the conversations wore off for each of them, they congratulated me and wished me well.

Still, I had no idea of what part of Arizona I would be interested in living in, or the fundamentals of how my vision would come together. I remembered that I'd had a childhood friend that had moved to Arizona decades ago. Did I dare to dream that she'd still be there? And if so, many other questions swam through my head: Would she remember me? I'd known her back in grade school and while we sporadically kept in touch over the years, it had been quite

The Change

some time since we'd last talked. I'd move a few times since then and I'd imagined so had she. In addition, I wondered if she'd be able to assist me in finding employment, searching for an apartment, or simply be able to advise me on what to do once I arrived?

I excitedly did a search for her on the internet. There was nothing available. I realized I'd been searching for her by her maiden name, but I couldn't remember her married name.

I began to conduct a search using the names of her family members hoping against the odds that I'd locate someone that would be able to share some valuable information about her with me. Still my search results ended with no success. I anxiously checked manually through my old files and rolodex and eureka... I'd located her married name! I plugged that into my internet search and all of her information blasted across the screen! She and her husband were now pastors of a church in Arizona and they were also avid volunteers in their community.

With some trepidation, I called the number listed for her. In my excitement, it hadn't dawned on me that there was a three-hour time difference from East to West Coast time zones. It was 8 a.m. my time—5 a.m. her time. She answered the phone in that groggy way people do when they've been aroused from a deep sleep. I asked if I had the right number for Pastor LaDawnna Hudson and she assured me I had reached her. I apologized for having awakened her and nervously stated perhaps I'd better call her back later. She insisted that she's always available for her flock and asked what my concern was. The conversation ensued accordingly:

"This is Sherry Brantley. I don't know if you remember me."

Her voice lit up and she exclaimed: *"Of course I remember you! You were my best friend in grade school! What's going on? Is everything okay?"*

Insights into Self-Empowerment

I then explained to her that I was planning to move to Arizona and wanted to know if she were still there. She excitedly told me she was, and that my decision would be one of the best moves I could make. She explained how beautiful the state was, how friendly the people were, and that I would love not freezing during the winter months. She advised me that she and her husband would love to have me stay with them in their spacious home until I was fully comfortable and ready to strike out on my own and she'd look forward to welcoming me with open arms! I was ecstatic. I was floored beyond belief! As it was five o'clock in the morning for her, she asked me to call her later that morning and she begged me to make sure that I wouldn't change my mind with the dawn of the new day approaching. I assured her I was sincere and that my mind was already made up to move. I told her that it was no coincidence that I was able to locate her and reconnect with her at this time in my life.

That Monday, exactly two days after deciding to move across country, I turned in my resignation to my employer. Was I nervous about the entire situation? Sure! But on that same day, I got a call from a major company with a location in Arizona advising they were recruiting and asking if I'd consider becoming one of their valued employees. They asked how soon I'd be in Arizona and after explaining I'd just turned in a four-week resignation letter to my current employer, I advised them of my time frame for relocating.

A friend stepped forward and offered to post pictures of all of my belongings on her bulletin board at work so that I could sell my furniture and household items quickly. Between that effort and posting information on a much-used internet site designed for selling items, I was able to sell everything and secure additional funding for my move. In conjunction with that, one of my best friends purchased my car. It was an older model car which I hadn't planned to take with me and therefore, everything came together to allow me to experience a smooth, stress-free move.

The Change[9]

As you can see, once I became firm in my decision to take action, universal forces aligned with my newfound belief system and my intentions. Immediately, opportunities to step up to the plate presented themselves for me to take advantage of. This reduced my stress level and eliminated my fears altogether. **Within a month, I was residing in the place of my dreams!**

You see, the universe supports us in our belief systems. Since no one can live beyond what they truly believe, it is imperative that we begin to take a look at said beliefs. All too often, people stay in situations that are unhealthy either spiritually, mentally, physically, financially, or emotionally, and rationalize this to be their lot in life. *Do not confuse poor decision-making with destiny* and likewise, begin to understand that what you're experiencing is what you're creating. Time and time again. You do not have to venture far to see what you have created in your life. Are you experiencing love? There is no such thing as 'genuine' love or 'real' love. Love IS genuine and real. If it's anything other than that, then you are identifying with something that is other than love. Are you happy with your place of employment? Do you have friends that care for you? Are you a person known for your integrity? Your honesty? Do you have goals that you are on a definite track to achieving? These are just some of the questions you'll want to reflect on to assist you in determining what you'd truly like to create in your life.

As long as I saw myself living in Michigan, dreading the winter months, hating to shovel the snow; as long as I didn't begin to create something different for myself, the universe allowed me to continue in that realm. But once I decided that Arizona was where I wanted to be; once I aligned my heart and my head with that desire; *once I took the necessary steps to begin moving in the direction of my dreams,* I was presented with the perfect opportunities to manifest that change. I was once again reminded: *There need be no delay between the mental visualization and the physical creation.* As my new belief system proved itself by being put to the test, I began to delve into the positive books and messages regarding the awesome power of my thoughts, actions, and deeds in relation to the very literal powers of the universal laws of attraction.

After committing to developing and establishing a new belief system for yourself—one that is positive, powerful, and pursued with your action—over time, you'll begin to *'physically create what you mentally demonstrate,'* and you'll experience a shorter timeframe between your initial mental visualization and your actual physical creation!

What will help you to gain a new worldview quite frankly, will depend on you. What inspires you to higher heights? Below is a poem from my book, *'All Kinds of Poems for All Kinds of People,'* which inspired me to remain focused, and proved to ignite the initial spark I held within me to propel me ever forward towards my goals.

THE LADY IN THE PICTURE

I had a picture taken and it turned out really great.

In it, I seem to rule my world, My power is innate.

My eyes gleam of desires, that boldly speak my truth,

My expression shows experience I've learned while in my youth.

My smile is quite inviting as I offer you a peek,

To journey to your own world, your destiny to seek.

I stand proud and tall as my "I Am' is proclaimed,

Envisioning my future—Living it, the Ultimate Aim.

Why do I view there, just a 'facsimile' of what could be,

Why don't I walk in its glory, to begin the 'Inner Me?'

Why does it face me daily, a reminder just to show,

The Change[9]

The 'Me' I want *to be—which I have yet to know?*

I must face all the challenges that have kept me cloaked in fear,

And make all my desires—concrete, concise and clear.

Because real goals need a time frame, an action *item for them all,*

It's time to LIVE THE PICTURE—and remove it from the wall!

Oliver Wendell Holmes said, *"Man's mind, stretched to a new idea, never goes back to its original dimension,"* and I say: It's a good thing it doesn't!

***

To Contact Sherry:

www.sherrybrantley.com

www.steppbook.com

www.inspirationalvoice.com

www.starttoexercisepersonalpower.blogspot.com

E-Mail: yourdesiredlife@aol.com

1-877-243-7043

Wendy Nagel

Wendy is an executive, leadership and transformation management consultant. She is a Professional Integral Coach through the Centre for Coaching (Graduate School of Business – UCT) as well as an Associate Certified Coach with the International Coaching Federation (ICF).

Wendy worked within the corporate environment for 22 years within the marketing strategy arena. Her experience spanned various blue chip companies, namely, Toyota SA Marketing, MTN cellular and banking (Standard, Absa, and Nedbank). It is in this context that she discovered her true passion for facilitating the discovery of untapped potential in others.

As an integral, systemic constellation and enneagram coach, her focus is on achieving full competence within the multiple dimensions of what it takes to be an impactful, mindful, engaged, and contributing human being or organization. Focusing on the quality of relationship with self (thoughts, feelings, and action), others, and systems/processes; she works with individuals and teams to organize themselves for clearly defined and measurable outcomes. The process is structured and aligned to specific purpose and outcomes, with the intention of developing skills and competencies for sustainable change in individuals and teams.

The World needs a Potential Revolution

By Wendy Megan Nagel

What is POTENTIAL?

According to the British Dictionary, one definition is "to be capable of being, but not yet evident." What determines whether potential is realized? Who determines this? Is it a product of nature or nurture? What role might choices and the right of an individual to choose play? If diamonds are formed under pressure, would it be safe to say that potential is realized out of pressure, challenge, striving, and sheer hard work? Does potential truly emerge when the going gets tough and resourceful invention/innovation/creativity is required? It is in this landscape that I find myself to be deeply curious.

I'm curious about how we choose to deal with the challenges of life and how these choices seem to determine whether we rise or fall, expand or contract, shine our light brightly or hide behind facades, roles, titles, _____ reader fill in your gap!

I'm also curious about the stories that we buy and sell, the tales we tell ourselves, that we repeat, believe, and then live by and how these narratives more often than not define the quality and texture of our lives. That we are responsible for creating our story, as individuals, as communities, as countries, and as humanity, can be a hefty burden to bear and as such the tendency and temptation may be that we stop actively participating as the primary players, choosing instead to become the victims or unconscious spectators of our stories.

Our challengers and protagonists represent our greatest allies, teachers, catalysts, and guides; and yet we shy away from them because to have our vulnerabilities revealed is painful and edgy. We seek out the comfort of a smooth ride without any bumps in the road and we become masterful at developing strategies to shield and protect ourselves from our truth. We marvel at the beauty of the rose, but scorn and avoid the thorns and leafy blemishes. However, the learning is that we are to acknowledge and appreciate the beauty of our potential embedded in the metaphorical rose as much as we are to note and guard against our thorns and imperfections.

Rumi's poem *Your Defects* speaks to this aspect of humanity so beautifully:

YOUR DEFECTS

An empty mirror and your worst destructive habits,

when they are held up to each other,

that's when the real making begins.

That's what art and crafting are.

A tailor needs a torn garment to practice his expertise.

The trunks of trees must be cut and cut again

so they can be used for fine carpentry.

Your doctor must have a broken leg to doctor.

Your defects are the ways that glory gets manifested.

This poem serves as a constant reminder, that we are born, we develop out of suffering, and we have the potential to manifest our greatness as a human in humanity despite our darkest hours, depending on the choices we make in these moments of despair.

The words of former South African President and Nobel Peace Prize Winner Nelson Mandela ring true: "I am fundamentally an optimist. Whether that comes from nature or nurture, I cannot say. Part of being optimistic is keeping one's head pointed toward the sun, one's feet moving forward. There were many dark moments when my

The Change[9]

faith in humanity was sorely tested, but I would not and could not give myself up to despair. That way lays defeat and death."

All that is required is for us to step into and own our truths, hurts, and our despair.

Our lives and what we amount to are nothing more than the sum of the stories we choose to believe about ourselves. And now for my story, which has led me to write this…

Eleven years ago I woke up. I had been asleep to my life for 24 years and so at the age of 35, I got served. Not in the traditional sense, that would come three years later…But in the sense that I got my proverbial wake-up call, my 'satori'—an abrupt opening of the eye of awareness. Some might be served a devastating trauma, loss, or disease, a cosmic slap, an accident or big red flag; but no matter your brand of wake-up call, it is always served cold with a stinging smack which gets you sitting up while your world is turned upside down!

I remain curious about the reason the extent of these smack downs varies so enormously from person to person, but I am increasingly certain they serve a higher purpose and we get dealt what we need to become conscious, fully awake.

And so in 2004, in my mid-thirties, the benevolent universe that guides and resides in each of us, and which I believe desires only the very best for us, ensured that I began a deep interrogation to understand and piece together the various chapters, characters, and themes of my life story.

There are as many of these stories as there are human beings on the planet, and the diversity of experiences are as universal as they are unique. Mine is and is not unique compared with any other's story and yet perhaps my response, perspective, and emergence out of it, and my sharing of my understanding to date, may facilitate a shift which creates new possibilities for someone else. So, here goes…

Having children had always felt like a seismic deal for me. It seemed to me to be the most fundamental reason for why we as spiritual beings take on the experience of being human. It represented for me the ultimate journey of creation: forging meaning, identity, inspiration, and responsibility. I had extremely high hopes of being a mother, nurturer, provider, guider, provoker, supporter, and inspirer of my children.

The process of conception took my husband and me over a year. A year in which I was pumped with fertility drugs, which turned me into a version of myself I barely recognized and would far sooner like to forget. In fact, the most narcotized and unconscious aspects of me were on full and glorious display: defensiveness, aggression, inaccessibility, neediness, and deep loneliness. It was a year in which I ballooned to a sizable 108 kilograms, which dialed up the volume of my misery.

I discovered that we had conceived on the 25th February 2004. The ecstasy and exhilaration I felt when I did the pregnancy test was unlike any I had ever experienced or had ever allowed myself to feel. Every cell in my body quivered with an aliveness I had long suppressed. I experienced a real sense of possibility and it was growing within me.

The gratitude I had for the soul that had chosen us as parents was enormous. In that moment, everything in my life seemed to be perfect and I felt valuable and worthy for the first time in 24 years. It felt like I was about to realize my full potential for the first time.

In early March, I was in my gynae's offices waiting for my second scan at nine weeks. I had insisted that my husband be present, as this scan would reveal the baby's heartbeat to us. As I lay there, filled with intense anxiety on one hand, and the greatest anticipation for the wonder of the process of creating another life, on the other; time moved into slow motion. The gynae was scanning my belly for what felt like an interminable amount of time, and with this my anxiety

The Change[9]

and fear started to rise like a stormy tide. When he turned to my husband and me and uttered the devastating words I instinctively knew were coming, nothing could have prepared me for the tsunami of primal anguish. I felt my deepest, darkest, and long-held suppressed hurts, rejections, and diminishments all rising to take a bow and an encore.

I do not know how I got home that day. What I do recall, is climbing into bed and crying me a river. It felt like all my possibilities and hopes had been shut down and a hopelessness filled the void left by my miscarriage.

Through reflection I have been confronted by the symbology of that scan. That day I was seeking the heartbeat of the fetus, and in essence what it was revealing was that I had closed off my heart, not capable or wanting to feel life with any degree of intensity.

I received tremendous support and love from my family and friends, and I stepped into therapy, which was thankfully compulsory, as I would not have gone willingly.

The universe, in its desperate bid to get me to pay attention to my life, had to resort to taking away something really important to me, in order to knock me off the predictable and destructive tracks I was on. Clearly I had missed many warning signs and gentle nudges until then and only in hindsight did I discern them…

Pause! Reflect

So, at this junction, I would encourage some reflection on what clues have you noticed or ignored? What do you feel and fear it would take to stop you in your tracks to receive your life lesson and to meet your heart's true longing? Do you even recognize its gentle tug and your soul's quietly persistent voice urging you to wake up? What signals is your body sending you? How can you begin to get in touch with what you really need and want from your life?

Therapy allowed me to gain a deeper appreciation and understanding for what had happened, and for my purpose. My work began with a realization that I had to start understanding myself (the beautiful, the bad, and the ugly), listening to my heart (it had been shut down on silent for a long time), nurturing and taking deep care of myself (what was the weight about?), and begin the process of a deep exploration and interrogation, to consider my purpose and internal motivation in this life.

To receive, this was the ultimate gift in my loss.

You may be wondering what had brought me to that point. I had always had a lively and vivid imagination and I always dreamed BIG, but something had me choosing to play small, being invisible, adding little value and not standing for much. In an effort to hide this vulnerability, insecurity, and low self-esteem, I managed an over-confident façade which created a world of pain; mentally, emotionally, physically, and ultimately, spiritually too. My life, to that moment, had not really mattered and lacked a certain fulfilment.

Losing a child made me deeply question the process of life and how it seemed that my unconscious patterns of adaptation to situations in childhood had moved me away from my fundamental potential. The work now was all about returning to that state of pure potential and essence. This for me is what it means to be human. We are born to parents and caregivers doing the best they can with what they know, and so our process of development unfolds. There is a pattern that is prevalent to me, in that we are born whole and yet over the course of our lives, we experience certain things which serve to fragment our wholeness and then, if you're alert, something occurs that ignites a process enabling a return to wholeness.

So when exactly did I fall asleep to my life? There was a very distinct incident that occurred when I was almost twelve years old which resulted in me taking on some spectacularly limiting beliefs. Yes, more than one.

The Change[9]

From the age of eleven, I unconsciously believed that:

- I could not trust my own feelings and intuition
- I was not worthy of love
- I was not valuable enough to be protected
- I was not entitled to speak my truth and,
- I could not ask for what I needed for fear of being too demanding.

The details of the event are no longer important, but the possibilities that I chose to summarily shut down for myself because of how I reacted to it created my self-limiting story for the next 24 years.

The deep understanding and naming of these unconscious limiting self-beliefs only emerged for me in 2013 while on a 10-day silent meditation retreat in India.

The possibilities that have emerged for me since then have been utterly magnificent and include:

- Forgiving myself for taking on my story of self-beliefs which limited my experience of life,
- Accepting and healing my addiction to food as my narcotizing agent and restoring my body to a balanced state,
- Forgiving myself and my ex-husband for the miscarriage and our failed marriage and,
- Realizing that I am good enough and deserving of love from myself and others.

It remains one of the beautiful mysteries of life for me, how when we are silent and still for long enough, that we are able to access our inner guru who knows just when to offer up helpings of deep compassion, trust, and a sense of knowingness.

In a moment of sublime clarity on day six of the 10-day retreat, I understood how I came to be where I was in my story and that the time had come to change the script. The real possibility and responsibility of being the author of my own story emerged and the questioning began!

I questioned everything. For 20 years, I enjoyed the trappings of a successful corporate marketing career across various categories of blue chip companies. I had the security I needed to feel safe and independent in the world. I had fortunately already followed some of the clues presented to me in terms of what truly filled me with pleasure.

These clues had kept coming in the three years post the miscarriage, in the form of Leadership Development programs that had me staring down the wormhole of my life, and the same themes emerged time and time again. I was more concerned for the people in my care as a leader, than the actual content of my job. I honestly didn't give a continental about how many of my organization's Home Loans, Credit Cards, or Vehicle Loans were sold each month. I tuned out of Exco meetings when these things were discussed and went into my kaleidoscopic imagination.

I loved nothing more than inheriting people that the 'corporate system' had disregarded, as it provided an opportunity to facilitate a process for them to realize that they had a contribution to make and therefore could find purpose and meaning for themselves. In doing this for others, the fire of passion started burning ferociously within me to achieve the same for myself. Amazing, how we do for others what we ultimately have to do for ourselves. Through these conversations with myself and others brave enough to take a good look at what was really going on, I took the necessary steps to study further and in 2012, I became certified as a Professional Integral Coach.

Pause! Reflect

Consider for a moment what you do so willingly for others? In what ways do you gift them? What if you were to offer these gifts so willingly to yourself too? What possibilities might emerge as a result?

The gift that just keeps giving

Off the back of the insight gained over the last 11 years, the most profound of which was realizing and understanding the self-limiting beliefs I had chosen to take on as a child, I took a deliberate decision to unravel my dependency on a corporate career, which had served me graciously for 20 years. I finally took action and consciously set about building an alternative career, one where it was all about empowering people to access their own untapped potential.

It took me two years, post my trip India, to realize this intention.

How did I eventually break free?

I knew I needed to be practical. So I began a slow process of thorough and careful financial planning which allowed me to see how possible it was to cut free of the ties that bound me to the delusion of security held in working for a corporate organization where my performance review document determined my value and then…I ran off a mountain!

Nothing dramatic…I was attached to a paraglider, but profoundly the mountain was called Signal Hill which rises gently above Cape Town harbor's Bay of Great Hope.

I had to do something physical and symbolic that would deliver a felt sense of what it would be like to let go of the old patterns I had mastered in order to survive to that point.

These outdated strategies were not going to serve me stepping into the entrepreneurial space. I could no longer be playing small, being invisible, compliant, feeling not good enough, or that my life didn't really count for much.

It is true that our adaptations serve our survival and success and so they are difficult to relinquish. However, none of these adaptations had me emerging from the caterpillar cocoon into a butterfly.

The paragliding experience served as a metaphor for trusting the universe to hold me and a realization that there is a connectedness in the system at large. A realization, that when things don't go the way we want them to, that it's a sign we are going the wrong way... I walked away from that paraglide with a tangible sense of what it would feel like to walk away from a marketing career and step into my purpose, and start living into my potential.

I have in the last two years been able to live in deeper compassion for myself and so a part of my healing has been the letting go of the emotional need for food and its addictive narcotizing affects. A whole food diet, regular exercise, yoga, and meditation form the corner stones of my self-care and well-being practices which ensure a level of vitality, curiosity, deeper connectedness, and availability for the demands of life and quality relationships.

Pause! Reflect

What practices can you consider to connect you more fully with yourself, your relationships, and your environment? What does vitality and self-care look like for you? How can you achieve these? And who or what might be waiting to support you?

It strikes me that we are seldom parented, schooled, or socialized to consider our imperfections and diminishments as being the way of growth and personal mastery.

As human beings, we are meant to stare down our storms, find and embrace our defects, and understand our true nature. We spend so much time disowning these dimensions in order not to reveal our vulnerabilities that we impede our own growth psychologically and spiritually. Our socialization teaches us that it is not acceptable to reveal these inadequacies. It's the ultimate denial. Instead, we are made to feel shame for our mistakes and our fragility in a society hell bent on projecting an image of perfection and success at all costs.

Perfection I have learnt, does not exist, but as long as we are striving to be better than we were yesterday, by our own standards, we are on the right track. You see, when we understand our self-imposed limitations and how they came to be, we get to choose anew how we will begin responding to them in order to shift our experience in the world.

It is this exact premise that I want to challenge in homes, schools, society, and the world at large. How do we start focusing on bringing out the very best in each other and so allow the best of humanity to emerge? How do we start to change our collective story?

Imagine how different the human experience could be if everyone could be more curious and compassionate with themselves? Where parents and educators consciously encourage a curiosity to understand and own our internal thoughts and feelings, so that we can be offering the most authentic version of ourselves to the world. By allowing this to become a reality, we are able to give courage to others to do the same. When we fail to acknowledge our diminishing patterns of adaptation, we move away from wholeness and tend to remain fragmented and limit our potential because we automatically assume that it is not possible.

These tactics, while they may serve us temporarily, largely act as numbing agents which dull our senses, making us less conscious with each adaptation and ultimately deny us and those around us our true POTENTIAL. Most alarmingly, these tactics prevent us from boldly confronting one tough question, namely, "What is my life really going to be about?"

Werner Erhard, in 2007, wrote in *Purpose and Aliveness:*

"It's funny, but when the ALIVE you emerges from behind the smokescreen of all those patterns [that block your aliveness] and begins to participate in life directly, life really does have purpose. It all somehow makes sense, in a fantastic way...Aliveness and purpose are practically the same thing. As more and more of us get to see that the purpose is greater aliveness, it happens that all of us start to do the same thing—we start serving purpose. Life comes on to us in our own terms, and so does the opportunity to serve."

Accessing our potential and bringing aliveness to this life it would seem IS our birthright.

Realizing your potential starts by confronting the fear that has you merely eking out an existence and gets you moving towards living a full and rich life. Stepping into potential does not always require a fundamental shift in life, but often a shift in how one perceives it and chooses to respond to it.

"What if contribution was about causing and generating a society organized around actualized power (creation, partnership and capacity to give life) rather than domination power (conquest, domination, and capacity to take life)?" (Eisler, 1995)

Pause! Reflect

What conscious choices do you need to make now in order for your life to take its future desired shape? Do you dare to dream that anything is possible, so long as you put your mind, heart, and body into it?

Imagine a world where each human being focused on bringing their gift to the world, rather than on what they will take from it. Imagine if each person participates in the game of POTENTIALIZED HUMANITY. In this game, there is a role for everyone. What will yours be?

To Contact Wendy:

Tel: +27(0)82 417 9559

Email: wendy@coachingforpotential.com

Web: www.coachingforpotential.com

Sidney Maestre

Sidney Maestre, is a self-proclaimed Spiritual Warrior who was a stockbroker in Silicon Valley, California. His journey of enlightenment led to the I AM teaching of *The Impersonal Life* by Joseph Benner and the development of *The Dalai Lama's Cat* movie. A movie which he believes can help the world face the serious challenges of today. He has plans for more films that "make a difference." Currently he resides in Las Vegas with his feline roommates, Sweet Pea, Julius, and Buddy Love.

I AM THAT I AM

My Journey of Trust and Faith

By Sid Maestre

Day 1 September 20, 2012

I started journaling to record my experience of discerning the "I AM" voice, the inner voice that is always talking. That voice in your head that never shuts up, that judgmental voice telling you what is right or wrong, good or bad, like or dislike, etc., yes, that voice. I planned to pay attention to my thoughts, consciously acknowledge their source, trust my discernment and, with faith, go where I am led without fear of the outcome. I believe there is a lesson in all experiences, especially when I think it is the worst thing that's ever happened to me. Basically, my goal is to live in the 'I AM' presence and trust that everything I do is for my best interest.

Day 2

I trust God to guide me in my daily living, thus my journaling each night will flow easily and effortlessly. The journal is my personal experience of heightened awareness and attentive listening which connects me with the impersonal God within.

The journaling of 1000 days has begun. Today I got an idea to write letters to my family and friends, asking forgiveness for various wrongs and transgressions that I've committed over the years. My parents and lovely ex-wife topped the list. Within a week, the list had expanded to 16, 17 if you count God. I had no thoughts of not writing the letters, or of censoring who was on my list. I know God's plan for me is to process whatever is in front of me and the details are insignificant. Good or bad, what counts is the lesson, as that's what my soul needs.

Day 4

My letter to God expressed gratitude for my life. I know that every choice I've made, every thought I've had, and every word I've spoken were necessary for my soul's growth. I now asked for guidance in serving others. As I finished the letter, I began crying, not your ordinary tears rolling down your cheeks. This was an all-consuming, gut-wrenching, take your breath away crying. Call me crazy, but I interpreted this as a personal spiritual experience with God. I have faith in my God thoughts, minute by minute, hour by hour, and day by day. If my story is helpful to your journey through life, than you're in God's hands, I'm just the messenger.

Day 10

Within the first 10 days of journaling, I discovered a technique for reducing negative and self-defeating thoughts. This was listening with my Spiritual EAR, an acronym I coined for letting go of negative thinking and beliefs. For example, let's take fear, arguably the biggest obstacle that we face. Fear comes in all shapes and sizes. Number one for me is "Fear of Failure," or maybe it's "Fear of Success." I'm still trying to figure that one out. You may fear what people may say or what they may think. You may fear you'll be embarrassed or look foolish. You fill in the blank for your fear, the one that stops you.

Returning to the Spiritual Ear, the E embraces the fear as it's real for you, without excuses or explanations, it is what it is. The A is accepting responsibility for the feelings you have around the issue. They are not caused by anyone else, as in, "You hurt my feelings!" Your feelings are an inside game. No one else is responsible for how you feel. The R releases and lets it go. The questions to ask yourself, "Am I willing to let go of blaming others for my reactions and feelings when I'm the one responsible? Will I stop claiming it is not my fault?"

The Change[9]

A persistent negative thought which I've lived with most of my life is that I lacked discipline with money. The truth of the matter is that I loved to gamble. I tried to quit numerous times, sometimes it lasted six months or a year, a few times even longer. That changed on February 25, 2011, a date easy for me to remember. As I drove home from a casino that day, I made the decision to stop gambling. Of course, I had no idea that it would be different this time. On more than one occasion I've been accused of being clueless and this is a great example. As my resolve remained firm over the following months, the lightbulb suddenly came on. I had been reading a book almost daily that was influencing my life in a profound way. I found it in the midst of organizing the lending library at my church. When I picked up *The Impersonal Life* by Joseph Benner, my curiosity was aroused when I saw it was copyrighted in 1941. As I was born that year, I naturally had to read it. It is often a simple thing or event that attracts my attention that leads to a significant change in my life. Looking back, I notice how subtle God can be in keeping me on His path.

The book is spoken in the voice of I AM, delivering a message to the conscious mind. You may recall the burning bush in Exodus 3:14 when Moses asked the bush, 'Who are you?' and the bush replies, "I AM THAT I AM." I refer to this book as an "I AM" teaching. The "I" speaking throughout the Message is the Spirit within, your own soul which is the Real you. It is your Self that points out your mistakes, your weaknesses, and is always guiding you to live up to higher ideals held in your mind's eye.

Day 12

Today was a watershed moment that gave my life new direction and meaning. I came across *The Dalai Lama's Cat*, a novel of a kitten that is rescued by His Holiness, and grows up learning the Buddhist teaching, which she applies to her cat adventures. Best of all, she narrates the book with humor. I read an excerpt which moved me so much that I broke down again in a gut-wrenching, take your breath away fit of crying. When I got my breath back, one idea ran through my head, I need to get this book.

Day 16

I awoke to another glorious day in paradise, which is wherever I happen to be.

Day 26

Today I found a copy of my Personal Effectiveness Checklist. It's something I've worked on over the years and never completed to my satisfaction. It addresses 14 areas of my life that may need some attention and straightening out. To name a few of them: balance my checkbook and keep it balanced, keep all my tax information up to date, clean my car and keep it clean, clean my office/ house and keep them clean, get my health in shape and keep it that way (teeth, eyes, etc.), get my body in shape and keep it that way, and my favorite, get up to date on all correspondence for my life. The bottom line, I won't have any more excuses, period. I'll be organized, efficient, and more productive when I complete the list. Or, to put it another way, I'll have my s… together. Oops, I meant I'll have my stuff together.

Day 28

Had an idea for creating a free workshop of what I learned by organizing and cleaning up my life. One technique I discovered years ago to overcome procrastination involved moving into a new house. I was downsizing, and after settling in with the essentials for living day to day, I still had 40 unpacked boxes in the garage. For about three months, I looked at them every day, all the while promising myself I'd start unpacking them over the weekend It's funny, that weekend never showed up. Then I got a great idea, I got out a sharpie and numbered each box. My plan was to unpack one box a day and in 40 days I would be through. It sounded better than the last 90 days when nothing happened. The coming weekend finally showed up, God was on the job, and I went out to the garage to face box #1. Here is my question for you, "How many days did it take to finish the unpacking?" Whenever I share this story, I get a wide range of answers, 40 being the most frequent answer. Everyone is surprised when I tell them that it only took me three days, thus demonstrating Newton's law that a body in motion, etc. Taking that first step often gives you the momentum to take the next step and so on.

Day 28

The journal entry tonight started me on an extraordinary journey that continues to this day. The cat book arrived. As I was reading it that night, it occurred to me that a movie of the book would make a difference in the world, so I wrote in my journal, "I'm going to contact the author about a movie." Where did that come from? Making a movie was not on my 'bucket list,' and I didn't know anyone in the movie business. In fact, the only thing I knew to do was contact the author or his agent about obtaining the screen rights. I learned later it was an option for the screen rights.

To recap my first month of journaling, I had written 16 letters to family and friends requesting forgiveness, written a letter to God sincerely asking for guidance, and now had a plan to organize all areas of my life. Even though I didn't know how, I was on my way to making my first movie. There were two things going for me, a Burning Desire to make the movie and the Faith I can do it with guidance from the I AM. I'll come back to the movie project later.

Day 33

I am so happy and grateful now that I found *The Impersonal Life* by Joseph Benner. At first I was intrigued, then my daily reading became a routine that continued for the next two years.

I discovered the book in February 2011 and read it monthly over the next two years. My thinking gradually began to change and I soon realized that this was the spiritual teaching I'd been seeking all my life. My decision to journal came from a desire to record my daily experiences from applying the lessons in *The Impersonal Life*. Possibly the journal would be the basis for a book, the chapter you're reading is the first step.

Now back to *The Dalai Lama's Cat*. After studying the I AM teaching for two years, I was ready to move forward with my dream, or shall I say my really Big Dream.

Taking the first and only action I knew, I sent an email to the author, David Michie in Australia, informing him that I loved the book and wanted to bring it to the big screen. He passed my name and email on to his agent and publisher, Hay House, Inc. When I told his agent that this was my "first rodeo," they referred me to Amber Entertainment, a London production company headed by Ileen Maisel. After an exchange of emails, we met in Los Angeles for lunch, another life-changing event. When I gave Ileen my card, Sidney Maestre, Spiritual Warrior, she sat up a little straighter and declared I'm a Spiritual Warrior too. We have been simpatico ever since as SWS and SWB (For Spiritual Warrior Sister and Spiritual Warrior Brother). We spent a couple of hours getting acquainted and sharing our vision for little Snowlion, one of the cat's many names. The meeting went well and I was informed the next day that Hay House and Amber Entertainment accepted my offer to develop the project. Just like that, I was a Producer.

After various legal documents were signed, we were in business. I hired a screen writer and soon had the first draft. Many months and multiple revisions later, we had to admit that our script wasn't working. After sending Ileen some ideas for a new script, with the intention of writing it myself if necessary, she found an award-winning screen writer in Jon Tilly. Jon read the book, loved it, and wanted to write for us. We gave him our thoughts for the new script, he came back with his ideas and we were on the same page. We hired him and he delivered a script that is exactly what we wanted. We are currently talking to directors. You can follow our progress at: www.DalaiLamasCatMovie.com

The following mediation was given to me by my spiritual advisor over 30 years ago. I studied it, read it, and meditated on it off and on over the years. My understanding was intellectual and shallow in nature. I knew the I AM was God's presence within me, but I didn't really KNOW the I AM until reading and studying *The Impersonal Life*. I now have a conscious awareness and relationship with the I AM.

THE FOLLOWING IS A MEDITATION TO ENABLE YOU TO CONTACT YOUR SELF, THE REAL YOU WHO KNOWS. PLEASE REALIZE THAT THE "I" SPEAKING THIS MESSAGE IS NOT SOMEONE OUTSIDE YOUR SELF BUT IS THE REAL YOU, YOUR OWN INNER BEING, YOUR SELF. TO FIND IT, LOOK WITHIN.

I AM extremely happy that you have understood all that you do up to this moment. The I is life, therefore, wherever I consciously am there is also life. Wherever I consciously penetrate, everything becomes vital and life-giving.

Therefore, that which appeals to you as you read, is the **I AM** of you. My message spoken to your outer consciousness from within is but a confirmation of the **I AM** of you (with which you are reading these words), with which you speak, breathe, hear, and talk, which you always knew within, but had not yet translated into definite, tangible terms to your outer consciousness.

The fact is **I AM** you, your Real Self. Your human mind has heretofore been so engrossed with the task of supplying its intellect and body with all manner of selfish indulgences, that it has never

Insights into Self-Empowerment

had time to get acquainted with the Real you—its true lord and master. You have been so interested in and affected by the pleasures and sufferings of your body and intellect that you have almost come to believe that you are your body and intellect, and you have consequently nearly forgotten Me, your divine self.

I AM not your intellect and body, and this message is to teach you that you and I are one. The words I herein speak are my **I AM** speaking to your outer consciousness. You must know that it is I who run your heartbeat and bodily functions. You are reading these words with your **I AM,** and **I AM** life. Be still and repeat this to yourself: Be Still! —and know—**I AM** God. For it is I within quietly waiting for this to dawn on you. Yet, while waiting, it was really I who directed your ways, who inspired your thoughts and acts impersonally, utilizing each thought and act, so as to eventually bring you and my other material (mortal) expressions to a final conscious recognition of Me, the **I AM** of you that is presently reading these words.

Whether you went straight ahead or strayed aside, or stepped forward or backward, it was I who caused you to do so, as it is I who am reading these words this moment to your outer consciousness! As I am looking out of your mind and eyes this moment, do you think that I am saying, "I am God and you are you?" Of course not, **I AM** you thinking whatever you're thinking, for **I AM** all there is.

I AM life, **I AM** that which animates your body, which causes your blood to flow, your heart to beat, your mind to think; **I AM** that which attracts you to pleasure or pain, be it of the flesh, intellect, or emotions. **I AM** the innermost cause and animating spirit of all living things both visible and invisible. There is nothing dead under a microscope! For **I**, the Impersonal One, **AM** all there is. **I AM** infinite, wholly unconfined. The Universe is my body, the stars and planets, and all intelligence there is emanates from My mind. All

The Change[9]

love that there is, flows from My heart. All power there is, is but My will in action.

The threefold force manifests itself as all wisdom, all love, all power (or if you will) as light, heat, and energy. It holds together all forms in all expressions and phases of life, be those phases creative, cohesive, or destructive. **I AM** is but the manifestation of My Self, the **I AM** of you reading these words, in the act of Be-ing or state of Be-ing. No, there is nothing that is not a part of Me, controlled and ruled eternally by Me. The **I AM** of you that is absorbing these written words or symbols is the One Infinite Reality. Now you know there is no individuality apart from My Individuality. All Personality shall soon fade into my Divine Impersonality, for **I AM** light, the Universal Magnetic Field radiation—the very light of you.

Shortly, you shall soon reach that state of awaking where you will get a glimpse of My Impersonality, and you will then desire no individuality, no separation for yourself; for you will see that this is but one more illusion of your old personality—old reality—all illusion! For **I AM** all there is in Divine Reality!

For **I AM** God, the All-Invisible Realm of Thoughts from which everything comes and to which everything returns, and in reality (Divine Reality), I fill every space that appears to your mortal eye to be microscopic or even invisible. **I AM** you reading these words this moment. You are to me as one cell is to your body. I animate every cell.

As for teachers, there are no teachers—only those who tell what they know with their **I AM**; the same **I AM** which is part of Me. The **I AM** within, your inner consciousness, with which you are reading these words, is the only teacher.

Most people you know, or are meeting, are unconscious or asleep! But do not speak too deeply of these things until you know, **I AM**. The **I** is life—invisible, immortal! Know as people speak to you, it is their **I AM**, their souls, speaking to you through their physical bodies. You are now initiated into the Divine Reality. Your life shall be wonderful. Speak to the Force at any time. It will answer from within, for you no longer need any other intermediaries. The Christ, Rama, Krishna, Buddha Consciousness is merely the **I AM** reading these words. Now command your personality, the illusion, to obey you, the **I AM** which animates you. Your personality, the illusion, is fading; for **I AM** all there is!

I AM existence and nonexistence simultaneously

I AM bound and unbound simultaneously!

I AM immutable, homogenous existence like the sky!

The idea of me being this physical body is extinguished!

I AM a portion of the eternal **I** animating matter as life itself!

This meditation is a gift from 'I AM'

***

To Contact Sid:

www.DalaiLamasCatMovie.com

www.I-AM-Teaching.com

www.PersonalEffectivenessList.com

sidmaestre@yahoo.com

Facebook: Sid Maestre

Mickell Rose

Mickell is passionate about helping others feel alive. It is her fundamental philosophy that freedom and happiness can be fostered through a transformative relationship between mind, body, and spirit. Over the years, Mickell has helped countless clients experience this transformation.

According to Mickell, "one of the most freeing feelings in the world is feeling healthy."

Bringing both technical expertise and enthusiasm to her work, she is on the cutting edge of food psychology, and has a knack for explaining highly scientific physical processes in ways that make sense to her clients.

Mickell possesses a strong compassion and yearning to understand human struggles at a deeper level than most. It is this natural ability to connect with her clients that really distinguishes her from others in the life coaching field. When Rose joins forces with a new client, she wields her knowledge, compassion, and determination to powerfully lead them through the process of self-discovery. She makes their goals her own. And she never gives up. This is because she knows wholeheartedly that, even in the face of challenge or uncertainty, there is always something beautiful waiting on the other side.

Take Care of Your Body So That Your Mind Will Awaken Your Soul

By Mickell Rose

There is a moment when things just click. When you decide to wake up. When you decide your body, your mind, and your life are the most important thing you can pay attention to, listen to, and take care of.

In March 2011, the love of my life was murdered during a random act of violence. I was left with a lonely apartment that was once ours and empty dreams about a life I had once imagined with him.

After his death, my thoughts consisted of all the things that he had talked about wanting to do.

Before he had met me, he had not gone after his dreams or taken too many chances with trying to build a life that he wanted. He was an amazing father of a beautiful daughter. He worked hard as a laborer, but had always wanted more. We fed each other's spirits and he always got so excited when he talked about the dream life he was going to live now that he had someone to build it with. His soul was lit on fire because we believed in each other. It pained me to think that he might have had regretted not doing more or taking more chances in his life if he had known that his life was going to be taken at the young of age 28.

Now by myself, I felt lost and scared.

We shared bills and expenses. He had made more than I did, so when he passed I got into some major debt. I made just enough to pay the bills and had $40 to spare for food. I had to cancel my car insurance and phone to be able to afford living. I had a car payment I was upside down on and couldn't afford gas to drive it, so I began taking the bus and train to work and to get around. I had a friend drive me to the Dollar Store once a month to get groceries and food. My dog and I lived off tuna and rice for months. I disconnected and avoided my friends and family. I was depressed. I just wanted to be alone. I didn't feel like living.

I was at my lowest point; part of me wished my life had been taken too.

If you would have asked me then at that moment what I had done with my life that was of importance, what I had done to make a difference in the world, I'd have nothing but an average story to tell of a girl in her twenties who was still trying to figure out what she wanted to do with her life. Those thoughts added to my depression. Looking back was at times more painful than looking forward. The only thing that kept me alive and taking care of myself was my dog Louie.

My past was very colorful.

In my teens, I struggled with body dysmorphia, an eating disorder, and severe anxiety problems. I got into the wrong crowd and started developing self-destructive and unhealthy habits. Some crowds I chose to associate with bullied me, but I stayed around because I sought acceptance. Within a few years, I had developed a dysfunctional yet functioning way of living my life that consisted of toxic people, bad habits, partying, drinking, and drugs. I became dependent on things and people outside of me to numb and distract me enough to quiet the screaming spirit that was always inside me. These habits and bad behaviors carried on for years, not realizing that it was only suppressing me from finding my inner strength and spirit. I was always searching for something that made me come alive, but never thought to turn inward.

The Change[9]

I seemed to have all of those characteristics of a girl who came from a broken home, but that was not my story.

My family was successful. We had a beautiful home with horses, boats, toys, and other luxuries. We traveled and had different properties in different states. I had traveled around the U.S. and out of the country. My father and mother were amazing parents and brother and sister loved me unconditionally. I was smart and I was raised with discipline and taught to work hard for what I wanted in life. I did very well in school, averaging a 3.5 to 4.0 GPA. I was the captain of the cheer team. I was given opportunities in my life to ride horses at a professional level and competed at world-class levels. I had always been an athlete and challenging myself. Yet, with all of these amazing things around me and given to me, I still felt empty inside. None of those made me feel whole.

At this point in my life, I still felt lost and incomplete.

I was overly sensitive to energies around me. I loved deeply and felt things and emotions intensely. I never felt like I fit in to a school system nor did I feel I fit into any system. I didn't like rules. I longed to know my purpose and do something I loved, but there wasn't a job out there I could think of that I wanted to do that I would like or be passionate about. I longed to know my purpose and discover it, but didn't know how to. My whole life I guess you could say I was always rebelling against conformity and searching for more.

Then there was my moment when things clicked.

October 2011, I woke up and stopped looking outside of myself for answers.

Five months after my boyfriend had passed, I made a conscious decision to stop living a life that I would one day end up regretting. I made a commitment to myself that I would stop living in fear and be brave enough to go out and find out what I was made of! I promised to stop living a destructive lifestyle, chose to get rid of toxic people in my life, and stop putting my selfish needs first and lead with "how can I serve." That was because after my boyfriend's death, all the material things that once held value in my life meant nothing to me anymore. I knew nothing tangible would bring me happiness.

Where did I begin? Jogging.

It was the only place I knew where to start. It was the one thing that made me feel good. My dog couldn't stand being cooped up in our apartment and was always waiting at the door asking to go for a walk. His want to live and explore life saved me. We started to go for walks, which always lifted my spirits. Those walks turned into jogs. I started listening to audio books and personal development books because music made me sad. I stopped watching movies during my free time and started journaling. I stopped being on social media before bed and started reading books. I stopped staying home on the weekends and stared getting out and getting involved in healthy fitness communities.

I began to detox, physically and materialistically.

My new liberation of feeling like I wanted to live again led me to face my reality: I couldn't afford to stay at the apartment I was at and I needed to downsize my life. My closet was full of excessive clothes and shoes I didn't want or need anymore. My car was just a piece of metal that was draining my bank account that I couldn't afford to drive. My apartment did nothing but remind me of a love that once was. In that same October that I started moving my body, I also detoxed my life of all materialistic things I had accumulated over the years.

I realized I was a financial sinking ship and I had to get rid of the things weighing me down.

My first step was to get rid of the financial burdens weighing me down. I turned my car into a dealership and took a hit on what I owed. I gave my apartment complex my notice, knowing I'd take a hit for that too. I took a lot of my clothes to a donation center and homeless shelter to give back and downsize. I sold all my furniture but my bedroom stuff. I found a room for rent in a house near the beach, within walking distance to the office I worked at. Within weeks of waking up and making those promises to myself, I fully detoxed my life of excess things and had moved out of our old apartment. For the first time I had felt I was moving forward with my life and my spirit was awakening.

Through the action of moving my body, my mind came alive!

I discovered my anxiety started to go away. I didn't need food to suppress my emotions anymore. I realized that when I used my mind like a muscle, it didn't have so much control over me. I started running my days instead of my days running me. My attention then turned more to my nutrition. I was more aware of how food affected my mind and mood. After eating certain meals, I'd feel a change in my emotions and found there was a correlation with my emotions and what I put in my body.

It was the beginning of awakening my soul's purpose.

For the next several years, I devoted myself to growth, self-discovery, health, fitness, and vitality. I began juicing on a regular basis. I tried being vegan and vegetarian, then back to eating some meat again. I started eating fully organic. I did fasts and cleanses. All which made me come more alive and more in tune to the divine spirit inside of me.

Food and movement was resolving my problems in life.

I started attending a beach boot camp and shortly thereafter was helping run them. A mentor of mine, who started the boot camps, and I grew that boot camp from 15 people to over 200 people every Saturday. It was a free workout that gave back to the community and helped people come alive! I did Muay Thai conditioning for over a year and I learned self-discipline through that martial arts practice and discovered how you do one thing is how you do everything. My life began to unfold into a beautiful masterpiece!

My story was being rewritten. Who I once was, was no longer.

I started helping at the homeless shelter and volunteering at different events. My part in the boot camp fed my soul and helping people push themselves mentally and physically awakened my purpose. My story and my past helped me connect to people. It helped me to help others deal with their own problems. Deep connections were made with people because I was living in my truth, which allowed others to live in their truth. No longer did I feel I didn't have a purpose. I had compassion and love for everyone I came in contact with and was driven to help them overcome their issues through coaching, nutrition, exercise, and teaching them how to take action.

Being of service simply lit my soul on fire.

Opportunities started popping up everywhere. Book clubs and masterminds groups I attended brought people into my life that saw my potential and my drive to change the world and they pushed me to be better and supported me in my growth. Those people fed my life and believed in my dreams. I was taking action every second I could. I was a rep for a protein company, then a vitamin company. I started doing wellness parties and teaching cooking classes to the locals. I taught that you could heal your life through proper nutrition and action at different seminars. I took as many classes and courses as I could fit in my schedule to expand my knowledge of the body and the psychology of food. Before I knew it, I had my own wellness company and was working with people, helping them heal their life through nutrition and mindfulness. I then became an educator at a local entrepreneurial school. I even opened up my own organic juice delivery business. All of this led me to flourishing with my own coaching business as a Nutritionist and Life Coach, changing people's lives for a living.

The Change[9]

Finally, I didn't empty inside. My dreams were now becoming reality.

I worked my butt off. I failed. I triumphed. I had so many let downs and struggles starting my own businesses, but I never stopped taking care of my body and my body never stopped taking care of me. This allowed me to run my days, even when I felt anxious and overwhelmed. I might have had let downs and speed bumps in my life, but I never stopped chasing what made me come alive.

Believing.

After taking action and healing my life, I knew I wanted to be a coach. I knew I wanted to be a nutritionist. I knew I wanted to make a difference in the world. But most importantly, I believed I had the ability to do it all and that was because of the people around me, my daily healthy rituals of self-care, my daily meditations, my nutrition, my workouts, constantly expanding my mind, and my drive to never stop writing my own story.

Everything in my life has happened for a reason; the good and the bad.

I have healed myself of a death of a loved one. I have overcome my eating disorder. My need for drugs or alcohol no longer exists, and my anxiety is controllable. I found my higher power. Passing this gift of knowledge that was given to me through pain and hardships is my purpose. That is what makes me come alive and feel alive.

I have discovered a secret.

That secret is if you take care of your body, your body will take care of you. Your body is a temple and its state of well-being affects your mind. If you pollute your body with unhealthy food, a lazy lifestyle, toxic people, and drugs or alcohol on a regular basis, your mind will not be able to flourish. Your soul purpose will not be awakened.

My positive lifestyle changes led me to discovering my purpose.

I would have never been able to mentally make it through the hard times I've been through trying to become successful at awakening my purpose without taking care of my body first. I don't believe I could have ever seen the beauty in serving people if I would have stayed in that toxic place physically and mentally.

My story that was once paralyzing is now my catalyst.

We all have a story. We all have been through hard times. We have all had let downs and tragedies. It's not what happens to us that makes us, it's what we choose to do with it. My story now empowers me. It helps me be better at coaching and it helps everyone around me to see the light in the pain. I serve to be a mirror for those who are in despair so they can turn their story into something that inspires them instead of something that cripples them.

Anyone can heal his or her life through good nutrition and mindfulness.

Thousands of people have touched my life and I've touched theirs through my coaching. My principles of moving your body, eating clean food, and using the mind as a muscle has awakened the divine in so many I've worked with. It's all about balance, action, self-care, and self-love. It's all knowing that to flourish in this life, you first must take care of your body so it can take care of your mind so it can awaken you soul.

We all have two fates: Victim or Victor.

One is the result of thinking that whatever you were born into and went through happened to you. The other is the result of realizing all things in your life are happening for you. My purpose is to help people see the later. I believe everyone can be victorious in their life, no matter their circumstances. My purpose to help others discover the light within their own story and within themselves so they too can experience that moment when things just click.

To Contact Mickell:

Website: www.mickellrose@gmail.com

Email: MickellRose@gmail.com

FB: https://m.facebook.com/mickell.raddon

Afterword

Life is always a series of transitions… people, places, and things that shape who we are as individuals. Often, you never know that the next catalyst for change is around the corner.

Jim Britt and Jim Lutes have spent decades influencing individuals to blossom into the best version of themselves.

Allow all you have read in this book to create introspection and redirection if required. It's your journey to craft.

The Change is a series. A global movement. Watch for future releases and add them to your collection. If you know of anyone who would like to be considered as a co-author for a future book, have them email our offices at support@jimbritt.com.

The individual and combined works of Jim Britt and Jim Lutes have filled seminar rooms to maximum capacity and created a worldwide demand.

The blessings go both ways, as Jim and Jim are always willing students of life. Out of demand for life-changing programs and events, Jim and Jim conduct seminars worldwide as well as created a global company in over 170 countries called Quanta International that allows anyone to benefit behaviorally as well as financially.

If you would like to hear more about how the Quanta Company can assist you in both income generating and personal development, please email our offices at: quanta@jimbritt.com.

To Schedule Jim Britt or Jim Lutes as your featured speaker at your next convention or special event, email: support@jimbritt.com

Master your moment as they become hours that become days.

Your legacy awaits.

Blessings,

Jim Britt and Jim Lutes